Leaving Violent Men

A Study of Refuges and Housing for Abused Women

by

Val Binney
Gina Harkell
Judy Nixon

(Women's Aid Federation England/Department
of Environment Research Team)

Published by
The Womens Aid Federation England Ltd
First printed in 1981, reprinted in 1988

Womens Aid Federation England Ltd,
PO Box 391,
Bristol,
BS99 7WS

National Helpline (0272) 428368
Administration   (0272) 420611

Leaving Violent Men

CONTENTS

1988 Foreword

Ten years have passed since 'Leaving Violent Men' was originally researched. Women's Aid has grown and developed, but many of the problems facing women who want to leave a violent partner remain the same. New priorities have emerged within Women Aid groups – there is now widespread recognition that refuges need to make better provision for the needs of women from minority ethnic groups, an area which was not covered by the original research. However in some respects the situation for refuges and for women leaving violent partners has actually got far worse. It is with this sobering thought in mind that we have decided to reprint 'Leaving Violent Men', as a piece of research which is still valid today.

Looking back over those ten years, what has changed? There are now over 200 refuge groups in England and Wales. However, this does not represent a real improvement in provision, since the housing crisis and steady cutbacks and restraints on Local Authority spending on public housing has resulted in women staying in refuges far longer before they are rehoused, making it even more difficult for refuges to maintain enough temporary crisis accommodation. 'Leaving Violent Men' showed that the difficulty of finding accommodation was the single major factor preventing women from leaving violent partners – but the housing situation has worsened steadily since then, and the effects of the 1988 Housing Bill are likely to be nothing short of disastrous. Despite the increased number of refuge groups, we are still far short of 900 refuges which are needed in England alone (this estimate is based on the recommendations of the 1975 Select Committee on Violence in Marriage, which also indicated that the recorded cases of domestic violence are only the tip of the iceberg).

The funding of refuges is also reaching a new crisis point at the time of writing. There is no standard of funding pattern for refuges, and groups rely heavily on the voluntary time and commitment of their women members. Many groups still have no grant aid whatsoever, or depend on highly insecure funding sources. They are heavily dependent on the basic income provided by DHSS board and lodging payments. These payments, however, are currently under review, and if Women's Aid refuges lose them, many groups will collapse.

In urban areas, some groups succeeded in getting five year funding under the Urban Programme and were temporarily able to plan further ahead in developing their services. However most of these schemes have now come to an end, and Local Authorities are often unable to pick up the funding.

Some groups, particularly in rural areas have been dependent on MSC funding for staffing – although the short-term and limited nature of MSC schemes made them very unsatisfactory. Now, however, the criteria for MSC are changing, and they will become adult training programmes rather than employment schemes. Another source of staffing for Womens Aid groups will thus be lost.

Financial survival for refuges has always been precarious. A large part of the problem is that responsibility for funding Women's Aid falls between local District Council Housing departments, and County Council Social Service departments and very often neither wishes to accept responsibility. There is therefore an urgent need for guaranteed statutory funding for Women's Aid groups, for at least refuge workers and running costs, playworkers, outreach workers and 24 hour telephone crisis lines. Such funding should be sufficient to guarantee an adequate number of refuge places, and satisfactory standards of provision.

'Leaving Violent Men' also examined the response of various agencies to women who have experienced violence. There have been gradual improvements in this field over the years, much of which may be attributed to Women's Aid's Campaigning work in condemning many of the myths and stereotypes surrounding domestic violence. However, women contacting Women's Aid still often express dissatisfaction at other agency responses. Legal protection through the Courts is also still largely ineffective. Police response still often gives cause for complaint although there is more awareness now, at least within some police forces, that they do need to improve their procedures and we welcome the steps that are being taken.

At the present time, the campaigning role of Women's Aid Federation (England) is of primarily importance, since so much current legislation is detrimental to women who have experienced violence. Under the new Social Fund, there is no longer any entitlement to emergency payments, for women and children trying to escape from violence. They may get nothing at all, or simply a loan, leaving them in debt, as well as homeless. The Poll Tax will make a women liable for her husband's tax as well as her own, whether or not she had any access to the family income. It is also becoming increasingly difficult for women to get Legal Aid.

Women's Aid Federation (England) itself lost its funding for nearly two years, but the determination and commitment of its members enabled it to reform nationally and embark on a whole series of important new initiatives: the National Helpline, training projects, housing and childcare projects and fresh research. Most importantly, there are still new refuge groups coming forward, and groups in England alone give shelter to over 30,000 women and children each year. Against all the odds, Women's Aid is still moving forward.

Foreword and Acknowledgements

The aim of this report is to show what services are presently being provided for battered&women in this country by statutory and voluntary agencies. The research, which was commissioned in 1977, was funded by the Department of Environment, but does not necessarily reflect the views of government departments. However, the report is the result of close collaboration between the Women's Aid Federation England and the Department of Environment, and the Minister of Housing has agreed to its publication. The three researchers worked closely with the WAFE research group throughout and also met regularly with an interdepartmental advisory group set up by the Department of Environment. The recommendations made in this report to improve the service to battered women have the support of all involved.

The refuge and housing needs of battered women and their children are the primary concern of this report. However, it also looks at the related issues of policing and social services, to provide a more complete picture of the needs of battered women.

The information presented here was collected between 1978–80. During this period and since the study was completed in September 1980, cuts in public expenditure have seriously eroded some of the already inadequate services offered to battered women. Despite increasing recognition of women's need to escape from violent men, the provision allowing them to do so remains poor.

We wish to thank all those whose help and advice made this report possible, in particular all the women and children who shared their experiences with us, and the refuge groups who took part. Particular acknowledgement should go to the WAFE research group who saw the project through from beginning to end. This report would not have been possible without an enormous cooperative effort from all levels of the Women's Aid Federation England and Welsh Women's Aid – local, regional and national.

We would also like to thank Judith Littlewood, Peter West, Rebecca and Russell Dobash, Jan Pahl, and the many part-time workers on the project at various stages – interviewers, coders, typists, computing assistants, book-keepers, photographers and printers. Special thanks should go to the members of Sheffield Women's Aid group, who were ready to rise to any emergency with all hands.

iv

*Women's Aid refuges rarely now use the term "battered" as it fails to give sufficient importance to the emotional and sexual abuse, as well as physical violence, that women experience.

Introduction

Violence against women in the home has been a common practice throughout history.[1,2] However, it was the opening of refuges which brought the subject to public attention in the 1970's. The number of women who fled to them showed that there was a hidden demand for a means of escaping violent husbands and boyfriends.

There are now 150 refuges* in England and Wales and they play a central part in providing emergency accomodation for battered women. Refuges are unique. Unlike hostels for the homeless, they offer a lot more than accommodation. They also offer protection from violent partners, mutual support and help on a range of practical problems facing battered women who leave home.

Two-thirds of existing refuges belong to the National Women's Aid Federation† This was formed in 1974 to unite Women's Aid groups in their campaign for a better deal for battered women nationally. It aims to improve the legal and housing position of battered women, to expand and improve refuge provision and to educate the public generally on the nature of battering and the solutions now available.

The extent of battering in the general population and the need for refuge accommodation is difficult to measure because of the private nature of the crime – it happens behind closed doors and women are often ashamed to admit that their partners are violent to them. Several attempts have been made to estimate the scale of the problem. The Citizens Advice Bureau in 1971 estimated that its branches dealt with 25,000 battered women a year.[3] Dobash and Dobash found (1974) that out of 3,020 cases of violent crimes recorded by the police in Edinburgh and Glasgow, 25% were assaults against wives or girlfriends.[1] Chester and Streather (1972) found that

*This number was traced for our study in 1978 – some have since closed but others have opened. The number in 1981 is roughly similar.

†Now the Women's Aid Federation England and Welsh Women's Aid.

v

90% of the 1,500 divorce complaints they reviewed in southern England were from women who had suffered "repeated violence in marriage".[4] Elston, Fuller and Murch (1976) showed that 70% of wives who petition for divorce each year "suffer serious brutality".[5]

One refuge place per 10,000 of the population was the level of provision recommended by the Select Committee on Violence in Marriage in 1975.[6] It also recommended other improvements in services to battered women: agency staffs should be "instructed in the remedies available to battered women" and more generally, "serious attention should be given within our school system to the problems of domestic conflict". Also that "conferences should be held up and down the country . . . to decide for each area what the best local response to its recommendations should be".

Our research was set up largely in response to the debate provoked by the Select Committee about the extent and form of provision to be made available to battered women. The study examines the work of refuges in providing for the short-term needs of battered women and their children. It describes the type and extent of present refuge provision and how adequately it is meeting the demand for refuge places. The study also investigates the long-term housing needs of women using refuges and the effects for battered women and their children of two recent pieces of legislation – the Domestic Violence Act, 1976, and the Housing (Homeless Persons) Act, 1977. It looks at the sort of housing women from refuges were given and how they were faring once they had been rehoused.

By investigating the attitudes and experiences of battered women trying to leave violent men, the research gives primarily a client-centred view of the agencies approached for help. It was beyond the scope of this study to investigate at first hand the viewpoints of the agencies themselves, but this has been done by several others.[1,3,7,8,9]. It must be remembered too that the findings throughout the report relate to women using refuges and we do not yet know to what extent they can be generalised to other battered women. This is the first large-scale study of refuge provision and the only study to concentrate on the attempts of battered women to find long-term accomodation. Alternative accommodation is one of the basic needs expressed by battered women seeking help and lack of it is one of the chief obstacles to leaving home. Its provision is therefore essential if battered women are to have any real choice about leaving a violent man.

Method

The aim of this research was to examine present refuge and long-term housing provision for battered women in England and Wales. The research was carried out in two stages:

i.   a national survey of all refuges in England and Wales and the women living in them;
ii. a follow-up study 18 months later of a sample of the women interviewed in the national survey.

i. The national survey

One hundred and fifty groups running refuges were traced in England and Wales in September 1978. Ninety three were affiliated to the National Women's Aid Federation and the rest were traced through Social Service departments.

Two approaches were used in the survey. Women living in refuges were interviewed individually, while groups running refuges or trying to set them up, filled in postal questionnaires.

Interviews with women living in refuges

Altogether 656 women were interviewed in September 1978.*

Table 1 : The refuges and women taking part in the study

Total No. of refuge groups	No. of refuge groups in which women were interviewed	%age of total	No. of women living in these refuges	No. of women interviewed	%age
150	128	85%	735	656	89%

*The count was based on the number of women living in a refuge on the interviewer's first visit.

Method

Eleven groups refused to particpate in the survey,* 5 refuges were either shut temporarily for repair work or had no women living in them at the time, while 6 refuges were discovered after the survey had taken place. Only women who had been in the refuge for over 24 hours were interviewed. There were very few refusals, women not interviewed usually being too busy with legal proceedings or other practical matters, which kept them out of the refuge.

The interviews were administered by 35 trained interviewers, who had experience working in this field. The questionnaire covered a wide range of topics – women's experience of violence and their past attempts to gain assistance from agencies, their assessment of the physical and social aspects of refuges and the problems they were having obtaining long-term separate accommodation. Interviews lasted between 1 and 2½ hours but in general women were happy to co-operate because they hoped it would help other battered women. The questionnaire was largely pre-coded but interviewers also noted women's detailed comments, which have been used in this report.

Ninety two per cent of the women interviewed were living in refuges, while 8% were living in a second-stage house or flat. Second-stage housing was accommodation groups had acquired in addition to their emergency refuge. It was generally used for longer stays.

It was decided not to include women who had not suffered violence but were in the refuge simply because they were homeless. Only 20 women fell into this category. These women were eliminated from the survey after a few general questions. Our findings are based therefore on 636 women, all of whom had left home because of some form of ill-treatment.

survey of groups running refuges

Postal questionnaries were sent to the 139 groups agreeing to participate. One hundred and fourteen or 82% were returned. This questionnaire covered the history, organisation and funding of the refuge group. It also recorded the numbers of women and children using the refuge, the amenities provided, and long-term provision for battered women in their area.

survey of groups without refuges

Thirdly, the national survey looked at the work of groups in England and Wales, who were either assisting battered women

*Reasons for refusal were usually that the group was too busy, or that they did not feel the survey was necessary.

without offering them refuge accommodation or who were trying to obtain some property for use as a refuge. Thirty three such groups were traced and postal questionnaires were returned by 17 (52%) of them. The low return rate is probably due to the difficulty of tracing such groups accurately, the tendency for them to change membership quite frequently or to disperse if their attempts to obtain a refuge are thwarted.

ii. The follow-up study 18 months later

The follow-up study was designed to find out the sort of housing women had moved into after leaving the refuge and whether they were having any particular difficulties after being rehoused.

A year after the original survey, all groups were asked to give details of those women interviewed in their refuges, who had agreed to take part in the follow-up.* Groups gave details on the length of time women had lived in the refuge, where they had gone on leaving and where they were living a year after they were first interviewed. Information about 411 women was received, and the results incorporated in the report. From these we selected all women living within a radius of 60 miles from Sheffield† for whom we had a tracing address. We also included a representitive number from London and East Anglia, to ensure that both urban and rural areas were proportionally covered. The number of women interviewed in each area was as follows:

Table 2 : Women included in the follow-up study

	Total in sample	No. of women interviewed	%age interviewed
Yorkshire, Lancashire and Nottingham	69	50	72%
East Anglia	16	12	75%
London	35	22	63%
Total	120	84	70%

Thirty six women were not interviewed for the following reasons: 14 women refused, 9 were traced but were not obtainable for an interview either because they broke several arrangements with the interviewers, were ill or temporarily away, and 4 women had moved to Scotland, Wales or Ireland. Nine were untraceable. Interviewers

*Very few women in the first survey had been unwilling to be contacted again.
†The research team was based in Sheffield.

contacted the Women's Aid group for help if addresses were out-of-date and finally Housing Departments if all else failed.

The sample was representative of the 636 women in the national survey on a number of important factors such as tenure, age, length of time they had suffered violence etc. The destinations of women in the follow-up were also representative of the 411 women mentioned above, as can be seen from the following table:

Table 3 : Comparison of destinations of women in national survey and follow-up

	%age of 84 women interviewed	%age of 120 women in sample	% age of 411 women
Living in previous home (with old partner excluded)	10%	6%	4%
Local Authority temporary accommodation	1%	3%	3%
Local Authority permanent accommodation	57%	40%	37%
Housing Association	8%	7%	6%
Private rented accommodation	4%	3%	2%
Friends/relatives	1%	1%	2%
Refuge/hostel	5%	5%	7%
Back with husband or boyfriend	11%	11%	16%
Other	3%	—	1%
Don't know	—	24%	22%
Total	100%	100%	100%

Over a third of the interviews were done by the research team, using tape-recorders to obtain in-depth material. The remaining women were interviewed by 5 trained interviewers. Interviews again took anything between 1 and 2½ hours.

The material obtained in the follow-up study has been used in the final chapters of the report on women's experiences since leaving the refuge. The illustrative material has also been used to supplement the findings from the national survey. The report also draws on other research in this field.

Conclusions and Recommendations

The extent and seriousness of the problem

This study shows that refuges are presently catering for a substantial number of families each year. The 150 refuges traced in England and Wales had accommodated an estimated 11,400 women and 20,850 children between September 1977 and September 1978, and had turned away many more. The women using refuges ranged in age from 17 to 70, and at any one time there were approximately 900 women and 1700 children living in them.

The vast majority of women had left home to escape physical violence to themselves and sometimes also to their children (27%). The assaults ranged from kicks and punches to strangulation, suffocation and drowning and were in no cases trivial. Other forms of ill-treatment women had experienced were mental cruelty and being kept drastically short of money.

Not only was the violence women suffered serious, but it had usually been prolonged. Women had suffered assaults for anything from a few months to 30 or 40 years, the average being 7 years.

> **Statutory and voluntary agencies coming into contact with battered women should recognise that the violence suffered by women was serious and often prolonged and was not "simply a marital tiff". They should also note that the violence tends to escalate over time and should therefore act promptly when approached for help.**

Responses to battering by legal, medical and social agencies

The two most immediate needs of women seeking help about violence, were usually for protection and alternative accommodation.

Although legal remedies for these needs exist in the form of the Domestic Violence and Matrimonal Proceedings Act, 1976 and the Housing (Homeless Persons) Act, 1977, in practice women had great difficulty getting the help they needed. Women had approached on average five different agencies in the past, ranging from solicitors, doctors and social services departments to the Samaritans and Gingerbread. However half these consultations had proved to be of no use. The agencies women had found most useful, were generally those in the voluntary sector, like Women's Aid and Gingerbread. In fact, the statutory bodies most in a position to meet women's needs for protection and accommodation, namely the police and housing departments, had been found least useful.

Statutory and voluntary bodies should note that the immediate needs of women seeking help about violence are usually for protection and alternative accommodation for themselves and their children. Where agencies cannot meet these needs themselves, they should refer women to an agency which can and should liaise with them on a woman's behalf.

Statutory and voluntary bodies appeared to be failing to meet the needs of battered women for two reasons. Firstly there was a lack of information about the options open to battered women. There was also a widespread tendency to regard domestic violence as a private concern which did not warrant outside interference, or as 'simply a marital tiff' which required counselling or 'smoothing over' rather than practical assistance.

The training programmes of social, medical and legal agencies should include the topic of domestic violence – its scope, severity and solutions. Staff should be well informed about the legal and housing options open to battered women and their children, including refuges.

Almost all the women in refuges wanted to leave their violent partner for good and our follow-up study shows that the vast majority of them did so. Only 16% of the 411 women traced a year after the interviews had gone back home. In spite of widespread acceptance of divorce and separation, battered women were being told to go back home and 'make a go of it'. This is often 'for the sake of the children', yet the study showed the children to have benefitted from leaving their violent homes, where quite often the violence was directed at themselves as well as their mothers.

Agencies should be aware that women coming for help usually wish to separate permanently from their violent partners. There-

fore, given the serious nature of the violence and the length of time women had usually suffered it, a 'patching and darning' approach to the problem is inappropriate.

Most women had tried to leave home in the past, on average three times each. They had usually stayed with relatives and friends, but these offered only very temporary relief from the violence, because of lack of space and harassment from their partners. By offering safe accommodation for as long as it was needed, together with the practical help and advice in an atmosphere of mutual support, refuges gave many women their first real chance to escape. The women we interviewed valued their refuge experience highly because of the unique combination of help and support it provided. This was not available in hostels, bed and breakfast or other forms of emergency accommodation. The institutionalisation often experienced in hostels was avoided in most refuges due to the fact that residents organised the day-to-day running of the place – often referred to as 'self-help'. Mental and physical health had improved while in the refuge and confidence had been regained. Mothers reported that children had benefitted from their stay in the refuge too. Most women were very pleased to have come through a refuge and felt that without it they would not have been able to make a permanent break. While improved implementation of existing legislation would go a long way towards making it easier for battered women to leave home, this would not do away with the need many women felt for the uniquely flexible and all-round help which refuges provide. However, a minority of women felt that they had not benefitted from being in the refuge and some other form of help would be more appropriate for these women.

Statutory and voluntary bodies should recognise that the mutual support gained from living in refuges run on a self-help basis was a valuable part in the process of women re-establishing themselves after escaping domestic violence. Improved access to permanent accommodation will not necessarily do away with the need for a refuge. However, battered women should not be forced to spend a period in a refuge before being offered permanent accommodation.

Existing refuge provision

The research showed that refuges were meeting an important need but were inadequately coping with the demand for places. In September 1978, refuge provision in England and Wales amounted to only one sixth of the level recommended by the Select Committee on

Violence in Marriage, 1975. While it is difficult to estimate the demand for refuge places, the evidence available indicates that there should be considerably more provision than there is at present. It is widely accepted now that refuges are dealing with the 'tip of an iceberg' when it comes to domestic violence[3] and that the crime occurs on a far larger scale than most people imagine. We know that wherever refuges have opened they have filled up and become overcrowded. Existing refuges are having to turn women and children away. In addition, refuges are unevenly distributed across the country, with large areas uncovered, some of them metropolitan districts. Few women were ever referred to refuges from areas without provision, which means that refuges are unavailable to women in large areas of the country.

Housing authorities should assess the adequacy of refuge provision in their areas, in consultation with relevant local agencies, and should support the provision of more refuges where needed. Authorities wanting to know what provision is currently available to battered women in their own and adjacent areas, might find it helpful to turn to Appendix A. For help and advice on encouraging refuge initiatives in their areas, authorities should contact the Women's Aid Federation, (England) at 374 Grays Inn Rd., London NW1, or Welsh Women's Aid, Cardiff.

The conditions in existing refuges

The study revealed that many of the properties used as refuges were unsuitable for the purpose and were in very poor condition. Most properties were rented from local housing authorities with no reduction in rent and half the groups reported that their refuge was poorly maintained by the council. This was made worse by the large numbers of women and children passing through. Of the 202 houses which had been opened since 1973 by the 114 groups in the survey, a quarter had since been closed down, either on health grounds or to be demolished.

Housing authorities should ensure that properties rented to Women's Aid groups for use as refuges are adequate for the purpose, are in good condition and are well maintained. When selecting a property for use as a refuge, local authorities should take into account the need for women to be near agencies they have to consult and should ensure that it is a safe and suitable place for children.

Most refuges were severely overcrowded. There were on average six women and nine children per refuge. Nearly half the women had to share bedrooms with other families, while almost all shared with their own children, whatever their age and sex. Refuges provided only the most basic amenities and these were in short supply. There was only 1 kitchen and cooker, 1 bathroom and no dining room or laundry room in most refuges. Women were highly dissatisfied with the overcrowding, the poor conditions and the lack of amenities available. However, most women were not in favour of completely self-contained facilities, because of the mutual support which communal living encouraged.

Some groups had managed to obtain suitable refuge accommodation, either purpose built or converted, usually from Housing Associations. Generally it seemed that refuges worked best when houses were not too large or shared by too many families – five or six families seemed the maximum. Where groups need to accommodate more than this number at any one time, this would be best achieved by the use of two or three smaller houses adjacent or near each other, rather than in large hostel-type accommodation.

The sort of refuge accommodation that would suit the majority of women in the survey, would comprise separate bedrooms, a kitchen and bathroom shared with only one or two other families and communal living-room and playroom.

The organisation and funding of refuges

Refuges were providing their services at very low cost, not only in the cheap accommodation they provided for a homeless group, but also by advising women and directing them to appropriate agencies. By meeting a whole range of practical needs, refuges saved duplication of effort on the part of several departments. Despite this saving in cost made by refuges, they generally received little financial assistance from housing authorities. Only 10% of groups received money from housing departments in 1978.

Half the groups had an income of less than £5000 per year to cover all their running costs. The major sources of income were rent from residents and sometimes grants from outside bodies. The existence of a grant for paid workers made all the difference to the work groups did. Although refuges were run on a self-help basis and did not require resident wardens or the supervision of day-to-day running, the sheer numbers of children and the help and advice needed with legal and financial problems, made for a workload that placed heavy burdens on purely voluntary effort. Only two-thirds of the groups received any form of grant funding for paid workers.

The chief sources of funding for refuges so far, have been the Manpower Services Commission and the Urban Programme. The former has now virtually disappeared as a source of funds for refuges, with only one group still obtaining money from it by 1980. Urban Aid is also only a temporary source of funds and is inaccessible to groups in some areas of the country. Refuges have now been running for almost a decade, they have demonstrated their importance to battered women and their children and the need for them shows no sign of decreasing. They should no longer be dependent on temporary sources of funding.

Local authorities should note that the experimental phase for refuges is now over and should offer them funding, as part of their main programme. Even when adequately funded, refuges still provide a much cheaper form of accommodation than hostels, bed and breakfast etc.

Facilities for children in refuges

Facilities for children in refuges were particularly poor and women were more critical of this than any other aspect of refuge provision. Given the large numbers of children in each refuge, the importance of such facilities cannot be overestimated. At the time of the survey, there were 1162 children under 16 years of age, living in 128 refuges. There were on average nine children per refuge, while a quarter housed 14 children or more. However, there was no playroom in nearly half the refuges and where there was one it was often poorly equipped. Only a quarter of refuges had play workers. A few groups had managed to set up the sort of facilities for children that the majority wanted – a well-stocked playroom, outdoor playspace and organised activities, including daytrips and outings. Only 20% of the under-fives attended nurseries or playgroups outside the refuge. The presence of so many children and the noise they made was the most unpopular feature of refuge life.

Women's Aid groups should see that Health and Social Services and voluntary agencies are made aware of the numbers and ages of children in refuges in their areas so that these children benefit from the facilities and services available.

Women's Aid groups should ensure that wherever possible, there is a well-equipped playroom in each refuge, and safe outdoor space for play.

The poor facilities for children were almost entirely due to lack of funds, although the unsuitability of the premises contributed to the problem in many cases. Half the groups had been able to spend less than £40 a year on children specifically and on average groups spent 25p a week on each child. Local authorities should bear in mind that the cost per head of improving facilities for children in refuges would be dramatically lower than, for example, the cost of keeping a child in care. Despite the poverty of their environment, children had more often than not benefitted from being in the refuge. They enjoyed having so many friends and mothers usually described them as happier and more relaxed than thay had been in the tense atmosphere at home.*

Local authorities should pay particular attention to the play needs of children in refuges, by providing playworkers and funding play equipment and outings.

Length of refuge stay

Although women benefitted from coming to a refuge, the conditions were totally unsuitable for long-term stays. The overcrowding and poor conditions began to get women down and they despaired of ever finding somewhere permanent to live. Most women felt that a stay of 2 months would be ideal, with 6 months as the absolute maximum.

However, because of the difficulty of finding permanent accommodation, women were having to stay on average 5½ months in a refuge, with 30% staying longer than that, in many cases over a year.

Local authorities should ensure that women's stay in refuges is kept short – ideally around 2 months. The present trend of lengthening stays – anything from 6 months to 18 months – should be reversed.

Second stage housing

Second stage houses are usually more self-contained than refuges and are presently being used by Women's Aid groups to house women who have to wait long periods for permanent housing or who find communal living particularly difficult.

Second stage houses are an inadequate substitute for permanent housing and should not be used to delay a move to a permanent home.

*A DHSS funded study[23] carried out by the Women's Aid Federation (England discusses the needs of children in refuges in more depth.

However, local authorities should support their provision, since it enables groups to provide a more flexible service to battered women.

Permanent accommodation

The Housing (Homeless Persons) Act, 1977 had improved women's chances of finding permanent accommodation. However, some women still experienced serious problems. 43% of applications to local authorities had been refused accommodation as homeless persons, sometimes because the Act was being ignored, but mainly due to restrictive interpretations which some authorities place on the Act. Contrary to the intentions of the Act and its Code of Guidance, women in refuges had been defined as 'not homeless', as 'not in priority need', and as 'intentionally homeless' or else had been told they were the responsibility of another authority. Only 44% of women moved into council property after leaving the refuge, although twice as many had applied.

The lobbying of councils by Women's Aid groups played an important part in eventually ensuring that some of these women were rehoused. But for others, there was little alternative but to return to their violent partner or endure long periods in emergency accommodation, in the hope of gaining access to the limited supply of private rented or housing association property available.

In some cases, authorities were insisting that women fulfil certain conditions before being offered a property, although they were homeless. These all caused long delays in the rehousing process. Women felt that having to pay off rent arrears over which they had had no control, or which had built up after they had left home, was particularly unfair, especially as most of them were living on social security.

Housing authorities should not make the rehousing of battered women dependent on such conditions as obtaining custody or divorce, transferring the tenancy or payment of rent arrears.

Few women in the survey wanted to go back to their previous homes but some were being forced by the housing authority to pursue this route to permanent accommodation. While 30% of women in the survey were trying this route to housing, only 8% were successful and a year later, only 4% were still living in their former homes. It was clear from the research that without much more effective protection, this was not a viable housing option for most women.

Housing authorities should not insist that the most appropriate route to permanent separate accommodation is for a woman to exclude the violent partner under the Domestic Violence and Matrimonial Proceedings Act.

The quality of housing given to women

A total of 63% of women left refuges to move into some form of permanent housing different from their previous home, most of it (70%) council housing. Their new housing varied considerably in type and condition. Complaints about poor properties were predictable – faulty wiring, damp, structural damage and a bad state of decoration. 70% of the properties needed work doing on them when the women moved in and it had taken councils an average of 5 months to do essential repairs. Some women waited as long as 18 months. Half the women thought their present accommodation worse than where they had lived previously and as many as 68% would have liked to move, either because of the area or the state of the property.

Housing authorities should ensure that battered women are offered a fair share of the properties normally offered to waiting list applicants who are family households with young children.

Starting again in a new home

After living communally in a refuge, many women found living alone with their children a lonely and worrying experience at first. Some were near the refuge or friends and could share child-care and have some social life. Others had been rehoused miles from anyone they knew and were still very lonely 18 months later. A third of women would have liked to share accommodation with another family after they left the refuge, but few had been able to do so. So although most women were very glad to have made the break with their partners, the quality and location of their housing made a great deal of difference to how happy they were in their new life.

More flexible housing schemes should be considered for this group of single parents. Housing departments should take account of women's needs to be close to friends, relatives or the refuge, when allocating them properties. They should also consider allowing two women and their children to have a joint tenancy for a larger property if they want to share.

The lives of many of the women in the folow-up study were dominated by poverty. Because they had small children, most of them were unable to work and were thus dependent on social security. Without better access to jobs and to child-care facilities or a better rate of social security payments, there was little chance of the poverty being alleviated.

The level of supplementary benefits paid to women leaving refuges should take into account the fact that they have often been forced to leave home at short notice and with few possessions. This report endorses the recommendation of the Finer Report on One Parent Families that there should be a higher level of benefit for single parents on long term supplementary benefit.

Many women had continued to be harassed by their ex-partners after they left the refuge. 11% of women in the national survey had had to leave accommodation in the past due to this. Because injunctions have so far not offered women effective protection, the most reliable safety measures were to be rehoused away from the area and keeping the woman's new address secret.

Agencies dealing with battered women should recognise that harassment continues to be a problem after women leave refuges and should therefore guarantee to keep their address secret from the violent partner, both when she is in the refuge and after she has been rehoused.

Women who left refuges faced a range of problems – social isolation, poverty and harassment from ex-husbands. Women's Aid groups tried to provide some form of follow-up contact, in the form of coffee mornings for ex-residents or by visiting women in their new homes. Some women also stayed active in the Women's Aid group itself, after leaving the refuge. However, lack of resources severely restricted the amount of follow-up work groups could do.

Social Services Departments should consider making resources available to Women's Aid groups to improve follow-up work with ex-residents.

Overview

Violence against women in the home is a social problem which can no longer be ignored. Overcrowded refuges across the country bear witness to the fact that many women are desperate to find a way out of violent relationships, and that the process of leaving is neither simple nor without humiliation. It is a measure of the quality of our society that we should not only accept women's choice to leave as a valid one, but also that we should ensure that an adequate means of leaving exists. The needs of women and children wanting to leave violent men can be met at relatively low cost financially. This cost must be weighed up against the misery and unhappiness of women and children remaining trapped in violent relationships.

1. Women's Need for Refuge

There is still widespread ignorance about the nature of battering and the form it takes. Agencies approached by battered women for help often have only a vague notion of what 'being battered' means. It is sometimes claimed that domestic violence has been exaggerated out of all proportion; that what are essentially only 'marital tiffs' are to be expected and should be dealt with in private. The embarrassment surrounding battering has frequently made it awkward for battered women to talk in detail about their experiences. It is only recently that the extent of violence suffered and women's need to escape it have come to light.[1,10] This chapter looks at who was using refuges, the forms of ill-treatment women had suffered and their attempts to leave their violent partner in the past.

Who was using refuges

The age of women living in refuges ranged from 16 to 71, and nearly half were under 30:

Table 4 : Women's age at present

	No. of women	% of women
under 20	27	4%
20-29 yrs	264	40%
30-39 yrs	224	34%
40-49 yrs	90	14%
50-71 yrs	51	8%
Total	656	100%

Sixty-nine percent of the women were married, 15% divorced or legally separated and 16% were single. In all, 8% had no children and the rest had an average of 2-3 children each.

The previous tenure of women in refuges is given below and is compared with that of the general population:

Leaving Violent Men

Table 5 : Women's previous tenure

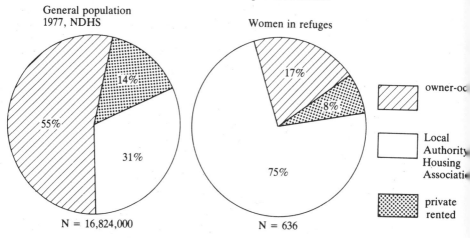

General population
1977, NDHS

Women in refuges

owner-oc

Local
Authority
Housing
Associati

private
rented

N = 16,824,000   N = 636

It can be seen that women from local authority housing were making more use of refuges than women from other sectors. This confirms the findings from other studies, [10,11] but it must be stressed that this does not mean that battering is more common amongst local authority tenants. There is evidence that battering occurs across all sectors of the population.

It is likely that women from different sectors tend to seek help from different social agencies and we show in chapter 2 that these agencies had very different rates of referring women to refuges, which may partly account for the discrepancy. There is also evidence to suggest that women from owner-occupied homes have access to a wider range of solutions in the event of being battered. The SHAC survey[12] of battered women seeking housing advice showed that those from owner-occupied homes tended to remain in the marital home and have their partner excluded, while none of those from local authority tenancies did so. Women from privately rented accommodation however, could be seen as the most vulnerable group in terms of housing and yet they are under-represented in refuges. It may be that women from this sector at present have fewer opportunuties to leave violent men. Clearly, more research is needed into the needs of and solutions available to battered women who do not use refuges.

Forms of ill-treatment

The majority of women interviewed had left home to escape physical violence to themselves (90%) and sometimes to their children (27%). Other forms of ill-treatment women mentioned were mental violence (68%) and not being given enough money to live on (20%). Many women had experienced several kinds of ill-treatment from the man they lived with. What stands out from the interviews, is both the severity of the violence and the length of time women had suffered it.

Physical violence

Severe and repeated assaults were something most women had come to expect and fear. Thirty per cent of the 84 women interviewed in the follow-up study had suffered life threatening attacks or been hospitalised for serious injuries such as having bones broken. Assaults ranged from being kicked, pushed into fires or through glass, thrown against walls or down stairs, being punched or having hair pulled out.*

> 'When he kicked me in the back, he broke a bone in my back – I suppose that was the worst injury, but personally it was always worse when he marked my face.'

> 'He threatened to kill me no end of times. He used to put ropes round my neck and try to strangle me – he even tried once with wire – that's when I left. The worst time he locked me and the children in a bedroom, put a gaspipe underneath and turned the gas on – nailed the door up with 6" nails.'

Violence was likely to be used against women for trivial actions which in some way offended the man – for example, not having a meal on the table the instant he arrived home from work, asking for house-keeping money or talking to the postman. At other times, something else had annoyed the man and he took it out on his wife:

> 'I was 17 when I first left him. I'd just had Paul, and my husband, he was violent – very violent. You'd get knocked about for missing the milkman or not ironing a shirt – that sort of trivial thing.'

> 'That time, he'd actually filled the bath up with cold water to the brim, and – this was all because he'd lost his money at the bookies – and then he submerged me in the bath; a cold water bath. I passed out in the bath, and thought that was it. I remember gaining consciousness on the carpet.'

*R & R Dobash' study of 106 women shows violence during a typical assault to fall into the following categories: Punch face/body 44%; kick, knee or butt 27%; pushing into non-injurious object 15%; hit with object 5%; attempted smothering or strangling 2%.

Sometimes the assaults lasted for hours and most women were too terrified to defend themselves. Women had been battered when pregnant or just out of hospital after an operation. In most cases (89% in the follow-up study) the violence had started only after marriage, or after a woman began living with a man, in a few cases on their wedding day.†

> 'It started on the wedding day actually. He took me outside when I was 5 months pregnant and he kicked me in the stomach. It were at the reception and he says: "I'll kick your face in if you even look at or dance with another fella." So that was it –I knew what was going to happen then.'

It was often only when the violence began to be directed at the children as well (27%) that women felt justified in leaving home.

Sexual violence was specially mentioned as a reason for leaving home by 4% (28) of women – they described being brutally raped, some as a result haemorraging internally or becoming incontinent. This is undoubtedly an underestimate of the sexual violence women have suffered, since women were reticent at volunteering such information to interviewers.

Mental cruelty

Sixty eight per cent of women said mental cruelty was one of the reasons why they had left home. Usually this happened in conjunction with physical violence. Some men had kept their wives virtual prisoners, not letting them out and insisting on controlling all their movements and knowing every detail of their lives:

> 'He was a very dominating person. You did what he said or else. You went to bed when he said, you got up when he said, you ate when he said, you went out when he said and you drank when he said. If you went out at night with him and you didn't want any more to drink, we'd get into the car and he'd tear down the road and then he'd slam his brakes on so hard, I'd hit my head on the windscreen.'

> 'When we first got married, we lived in flats and he used to lock me in for 3 days and I never used to see him and then he used to come back and hit me and say I'd had somebody in, and we lived on the 9th floor!'

Some women had been verbally tormented and threatened, until they were confused about their own sanity. Ten per cent of women had suffered mental cruelty on its own. This could be as debilitating as physical attacks, but women found it more difficult to gain

---

†R & R Dobash found that the beatings began only after marriage in 77% of the cases.

sympathy or help, as there were no black eyes or broken bones to prove it. One of the effects of this type of violence, was to destroy women's confidence in their ability to leave home at all.

How long women had been battered

Not only was the violence women had suffered severe, but it had often gone on for a considerable length of time. The average length of time women had suffered was 7 years, ranging from a few months to 30 or 40 years:

Table 6 : Length of time battered

	No. of women	%age of women
Less than 3 years	172	27%
3 to under 6 years	165	26%
6 to under 10 years	140	22%
10 years or more	159	25%
Total	636	100%

As the violence had usually started when women were in their early 20s it was generally the case that the older a woman was, the longer she had suffered. Most women had wanted to leave their violent partner from within the first year of the violence. Other research[1] has shown that the severity of the violence tends to increase over the course of the relationship. It is therefore disturbing that, although refuges have been in existence for 7 years, many of these women had only just found out about them. A considerable proportion of the violence has begun relatively recently, so there is no evidence that this practice is dying out.

Living in poverty

Twenty per cent of women said one of their reasons for leaving home was that their partner had kept them in extreme poverty, regardless of how much he was earning. These men spent only a fraction of their income on their families and seemed to regard their earnings purely as pocket money to be spent on their own leisure. Only a third of the women had had any sort of job before leaving home, often part-time. So most women were either wholly or partly dependent on their husband or boyfriend for material resources. Those at home with very young children were particularly vulnerable.

'The giro was in his name. That's why a hell of a lot of beatings go on, especially when people are on the dole – because the husband gets the giro and he knows he's stronger than her, she's got to get it off him. Can you imagine trying to get it off them outside the Post Office – you give them a dirty look and they just laugh. Mike used to get the giro, go to the buffet bar till 2, then the club from 2 tii 7, then the pub from 7.30 till 11, and then the Mermaid, which ended at 2.00 a.m. All our food money, half our rent. Used to do this from Thursday to Sunday and then we'd starve till the end of the week.'

Despite the low level of social security payments (see chapter 10), over a third of women living in refuges said they were financially better off on social security than they had been with their husbands. A further third said they had been no better off before than they were now. This shows the level of poverty in which some women and children were forced to live. Women who had been given meagre amounts for housekeeping, were sometimes forced to spend most of it on steak and such like for their husbands, while they and their children ate sausages or milk and biscuits.

Jan Pahl's work on income control in the family[13] shows that a family's standard of living cannot automatically be deduced from the bread-winner's income. A wife and children can live in dire poverty, no matter what the income of the husband and this may be a form of ill-treatment which has so far been seriously overlooked.

Leaving violent men – where women went in the past

With such ill-treatment, why did women stay in the relationships so long? Most of the women interviewed said that they wanted to leave their violent partners within a year or so of the violence starting. The majority had left before, on average three times, and some women so often that they couldn't remember. The question is therefore not only why women stayed with violent men, but why they returned to them after leaving. The main reasons women gave for returning home in the past were:

Table 7 : Reasons women had returned to violent partners in the past*

59% ■ ■ ■ ■ ■ ■	Problems with accommodation
56% ■ ■ ■ ■ ■ ■	to give partner another chance
30% ■ ■ ■	for the sake of the children
15% ■	forced back

The most powerful constraint against leaving had been the lack of somewhere to go, either immediately or in the long term. But other factors also played a part.

*Women could give more than one reason for staying or going back, so there is some overlap.

Once more on the run, this family has had its refuge discovered.

Problems with accommodation

The sources of accommodation women had used in the past and before they came to the refuge this time, are shown below:-

Table 8 : Where women had stayed on leaving violent men

	in the past	before they came to refuge this time†
relatives	65%	34%
friends	37%	23%
refuges	25%	26%
homeless hostels	12%	3%
bed and breakfast	9%	–
own sparate accommodation	11%	–

Relatives and friends were by far the most common sources of accommodation for women leaving violent partners, both in the past and on this occasion. However, they usually only offered a temporary breathing space to women, rather than the opportunity to make a permanent break. There was seldom enough room for a woman with her children to stay for long and she was easily found by her husband or boyfriend. The importance of keeping her whereabouts secret was clear from the pressures that came into play once she was found. Although some women had genuinely sought a reconciliation, all too often women described simply being worn down by their husband's persuasions to return. A proportion had literally been forced back--physically or because of threats – while others did not want to impose their husband's behaviour on their friends or relatives:

> 'I went to my parents and of course, he came – I left him because of his hitting and kicking me – and I went home to them, but he came there and I had to go. I went back really to keep the peace because my parents weren't able to cope with it.'

Finding temporary accommodation was even more difficult if women had no friends or relatives on hand to turn to. Thirty six per cent of women had never stayed with relatives in the past and altogether, 14% had been entirely dependent on formal sources of accommodation. Some women described spending nights in telephone boxes or public lavatories after violent attacks, others had left home not knowing where they would end up that night. The desperation and uncertainty of leaving home, are poignantly expressed in one women's story:

†Half the women had stayed in at least one place before arriving at the refuge, on leaving this time.

'I ran out the back door and all I had on was my knickers and bra, but he'd kicked me so bad, I couldn't go back. So I managed to pull an overall off the line. I ran in such a panic and I ran and I ran along the main road, and this car stopped and asked me where I wanted to go, so I asked where they were going. It was Carlisle, so I said, "Can I go there too?"With it being dark, they didn't realise the state I was in, so I got to Carlisle and was dropped off and just sat on a park bench. I didn't know where I was, I had no money, I had no coat. It was absolutely freezing, I had no shoes and no socks, I had nothing on at all and I sat there for 4 or 5 hours. The daylight had come and people were passing me and they must have thought I was mental or something like that. But I was in such agony and such pain that I just wanted the ground to open up and die.'

Even those women who had found temporary accommodation in the past had not necessarily been able to leave permanently. In hostels and bed and breakfast they were isolated and had received little help in obtaining long-term accommodation. Also, although refuges offered help and personal support, they were often over-crowded and women had had to wait for long periods in them without being assured of permanent accommodation. Even so, many women felt for the first time that by finding a refuge, they had a real chance of making a break.

Hopes that the man's behaviour might change

Women found it difficult in the past to admit that the relationship had totally broken down. Although the violence they had suffered was frequently severe, it had often been intermittent – there were good times as well as bad, and in the lulls between the assaults, reconciliations often took place and promises were made that there would be no more violence. Men were often very persistent in their attempts to persuade women to return home after they had left. Women were offered 'heaven on earth': washing machines, prams and reformed characters, if only they would return home and give men 'another chance'. Altogether 56% of women said they were persuaded back or that they went back because they felt some affection or hoped the man might change:

'I went back after 2 weeks. I fell for all the soft stuff – "I love you, come home". I fell for the trap.'

'I always went back after his promise that he would change. He threatened suicide and I got frightened of the consequences if I stayed away.'

Staying for the sake of the children

The belief that children need two parents put pressure on women to remain in the relationship even when it was a violent one. Forty three per cent of women had stayed in violent relationships partly for this reason and 30% of those who had left in the past went back for the sake of the children:

'There was nowhere to go with the children. They need both parents, particularly the boys – they need a father.'

'I thought he'd change because he wasn't violent between the beatings. I didn't want to break up the home for my daughter's sake.'

There were practical difficulties where women had several children. Bed and breakfast, hotels or floor space at a friend's were not the best places for children and leaving home often meant changing schools, moving from friends and generally disrupting children's lives, which women were loth to do. The responsibility for caring for their children entirely alone also made many women anxious about leaving: "I didn't think I could cope with them on my own, never being able to have a break."

Confusion about financial assistance from the state had led some women to stay put, believing that they were not eligible. Other women had baulked at the prospect of living on social security for any length of time. This worry was quite realistic. The Finer Report[14] showed that single parent families headed by women were one of the most impoverished groups in Britain. The idea of living on the poverty line was obviously a strong deterrent against leaving a violent man in those cases where his financial provision for the family was adequate.

Some women had stayed or returned home simply out of fear of their partner. Nine per cent said they had stayed out of fear, while 15% admitted that they had been forced to stay against their will or to keep the peace:

"I was too frightened to leave him. He said he'd do time for me – kill me. It wasn't for the children's sake – just because I was so frightened.'

As we see in Chapter 10, women were not free of this sort of fear, even when they had escaped. Eleven per cent of women had found separate accommodation in the past, and had had to seek refuge from their previous partners again.

Summary

This chapter has described the sort of violence experienced by women who come to refuges. The women had been the victims of various forms of ill-treatment, almost always including physical violence and over a considerable length of time. Most women had wanted to leave almost as long as they had suffered the violence but had been prevented from doing so mainly by the lack of alternative accommodation. Without it, there was little chance of women making a permanent break from their violent partner.

2. Women's Attempts to Gain Help in the Past

With such levels of violence being suffered, who had women turned to for help in the past and how useful had they been? In this chapter we look at the role of statutory and voluntary agencies in helping battered women. What emerges is that battered women had sought help from a wide range of sources but there was a large disparity in the usefulness of the various agencies. Whether an agency was useful to battered women seemed to depend both on its overall policy towards battering and the discretion of individual officers. The two kinds of help women most wanted were protection from violence and alternative accommodation. However it was clear that this sort of practical assistance was very often not forthcoming and that there is considerable room for improvement in the way most agencies respond to battering.

The number of agencies approached by battered women and their usefulness

The extent to which women had been able to gain the help they needed is reflected both in the number of different agencies they had approached in the past and the high proportion who felt these agencies had not proved useful. Firstly, the number of agencies approached:

Table 9 : number of different sources of help contacted in the past

No. of different sources of help approached*	No. of women	%age of women
0	9	1
1–3	185	29
4–6	271	43
7–9	147	23
10–13	24	4
	636	100%

*Contact with any source has been counted as one contact no matter how many times each was approached. See Table 10 for list of sources.

The average number of agencies or individuals approached for help was 5. In total 3,090 agency consultations had been made by the battered women in our survey, but half of these consultations were of no use. Surprisingly, the average number of different agencies contacted remained the same no matter how long a woman had suffered violence. This suggests that repeated failure to gain the type of help needed left women feeling demoralized.

One of the present inadequacies of agencies is that they do not usually liaise with each other on behalf of battered women. As Dawson and Farragher point out, a battered woman is thus "placed in the situation of having to start afresh with each new agency", and "the help she receives will be unco-ordinated and will not be cumulative".[3]

Their study found that the number of contacts between agencies on behalf of women was small – 1.5 contacts per woman – and no contacts at all were made for about a third of the women. As many women had reservations about admitting that they were suffering domestic violence because of embarrassment and fear of repercussions from their violent partner, such agency responses as these are unlikely to encourage women to make further requests for help.

From our own and other studies, there appear to be two main sorts of help women need from agencies. The first is emergency accommodation. If this need cannot be met, either by the agency approached or through referral to an agency that can, battered women will frequently regard the contact as unhelpful. The other most vital need for battered women is protection from the violence itself, for which women usually approached the police or solicitors.

The following table shows the number of women who contacted various agencies for help and whether they found them useful or not. Apart from informal sources of help, the three agencies most frequently contacted were Police, Social Services and Doctors. As can be seen, no agency was both highly consulted *and* useful to most women. Indeed, the very agencies who were regarded as most useful by battered women were less well-known, e.g. Women's Aid, Gingerbread. The two agencies most able to meet women's needs for protection and accommodation, i.e. the Police and Housing Departments, were found to be least useful by women. These and other agencies are examined in more detail over:

Leaving Violent Men

Table 10 : Individuals and agencies approached for help and their usefulness

Sources of Help	No. of women contacting them	%age of women who contacted them	%age of these who found contact useful*
Informal:			
Relatives	394	62%	61%
Friends	311	49%	58%
Formal:			
Statutory agencies			
Police	388	61%	36%
Social Services	343	54%	52%
Doctors	330	52%	56%
Solicitor	299	47%	66%
Housing Department	216	34%	29%
Health Visitor	146	23%	55%
Probation Service	95	15%	59%
Voluntary agencies			
Samaritans	146	23%	59%
Citizens' Advice Bureau	140	22%	66%
Women's Aid	133	21%	80%
Minister/Priest	70	11%	71%
Marriage Guidance	50	8%	33%
Gingerbread	25	4%	79%

The police

More women had contacted the police than any other agency, but as many as 64%† of these women had not found the police useful. The most frequent complaint was that the police were unwilling to intervene because it was a 'domestic dispute':

> 'When we lived in Newark he hit me all over – I was black. I was very frightened. I ran out of the house to the phone box – I was really petrified. The police came and just sat me in the car outside and said, "Look, you've got a nice house, you're a young couple, kiss and make up. Be friends".'

In other cases women claimed that the police did not believe they had been beaten up or else had openly sided with the husband. Sometimes the police simply did not turn up when called out.

*These figures apply to women who had suffered violence for 5 years or less so as to give up-to-date responses by agencies. The figures vary little, however, from those for the whole sample.

†A similar result to that found by Jan Pahl (63%), in her study of Canterbury Refuge, *A Refuge for Battered Women*, 1978, p.37.[10]

Police response to calls of domestic violence was investigated in more detail during the follow-up interviews of 84 women a year later. 59 of these women had called the police after the worst assault made on them and the police response on that occasion was described as follows:

Table 11 : Police response to call for help after worst assault

	No. of women	% of women
Did not come to scene of violence	5	8%
Said it was 'domestic dispute' – so no practical help given	30	51%
Man charged with assault or with breaking injunction	10	17%
Practical help given – woman referred to refuge or man taken away for night	12	20%
Other	2	4%
Total:	59	100%

Of the 25 cases (42%) of severe assault* only 5 of the men (20%) had been charged. There was even less chance of the men being charged where the violence was not what police officers term 'excessive'. Thirty four women (55%) had suffered severe bruising, black eyes and other injuries not requiring hospital treatment, but only 5 of the men (15%) were charged.

None of the men in these 59 cases had been imprisoned, although one received a suspended prison sentence. Fines sometimes had been imposed, ranging from £20 to £200, but they were regarded as an ineffective deterrent by most of the women interviewed. The men were left free to assault them again and the fines were often disregarded or left for the woman to pay:

'He was charged with Actual Bodily Harm, common assault and unlawful assault. He got fined, bound over and was given a suspended sentence. It was useless because he wouldn't pay the fine and I had to. They threatened to take the furniture if I didn't. And it didn't stop him beating me.'

Less than a quarter of the women in the follow-up study were satisfied with the way the police had dealt with their partner's violence. What then should the police be doing?†

There appears to be a dilemma within the police force about how to approach domestic violence. Research by Farragher[15] and police evidence to the Select Committee on Violence in Marriage[6] reveal that sometimes a 'peace keeping' role was stressed and at other times

*Involving life-threatening attacks e.g. strangulation, drowning or resulting in hospitalisation.
†For a fuller discussion of the role of the police in domestic violence see Farragher[15] or Jeffrey and Pahl.[8]

a 'law-enforement' role. R & R Dobash[1] quote a police training manual, which states:

> 'Once inside the home, the officers sole role is to preserve the peace . . . In dealing with family disputes the power of arrest should be excercised as a last resort. The officer should never create a police problem when there is only a family problem existing.'[6]

Farragher's study showed that a substantial minority of officers (40%) shared this view, while 47% said they would enforce the law against assault regardless of the domestic situation.

The main legislation covering all types of assault is the Offences Against the Persons Act 1861. The classification of assaults ranges from Common Assault, with a maximum prison sentence of 2 months or a fine of £50, to Grievous Bodily Harm with Intent, with a maximum penalty of life imprisonment. The police argue that in many cases of domestic violence, there is insufficient evidence of assault or else the assault is not serious enough to warrant action being taken.[8] Lack of evidence is indeed a problem since there are seldom witnesses to the event and sometimes the injury is not visible. Bruising does not always show immediately and some men are careful to hit where it does not show easily, for example on the head.

Farragher confirms too that many of the domestic calls police made involve heated arguments rather than physical violence. However, he does suggest that this colours police attitude to all domestic calls, including those involving violence. Our own research backs up that of Pahl,[8] Farragher[15] and R & R Dobash,[1] in suggesting that police officers' perception of what constitutes serious assault is influenced by their belief that what happens within a marriage is private and that domestic violence is different from other assaults.

The Bedfordshire Police Report shows that charges were not pressed in more than half the cases to which the police were called. The police argue that this is because the women themselves are unwilling to pursue the case. Jan Pahl's research points out that this is sometimes the case due to fear of retribution if they remain in the same house as the man. But our own research and that of Farragher would indicate that police officers' behaviour at the time can strongly discourage women from pursuing a complaint. Some women in our survey were not told that they could press charges themselves. The police have the powers to charge the man themselves and it is not always essential for the woman to even act as witness. Men frequently plead guilty on such charges thereby doing away with the need for witnesses.

The police also claim that women tend to withdraw the charges before the case comes to court.[8] This is not borne out by either the Bedfordshire Police Report, 1976,[5] where only 6% of charges were withdrawn, or by R & R Dobash,[6] who found that out of 933 cases, in Glasgow and Edinburgh less than 6% of the women dropped the charges. Similarly, Dawson and Farragher[7] found that there were only 8 withdrawals out of a total of 96 substantiated complaints of assault in the Newcastle and Stoke area in 1976.

The recognition that battered women were failing to be adequately protected under existing criminal law, led to the passing of the Domestic Violence and Matrimonial Proceedings Act in 1976. In theory, injunctions protect women by restraining the partner from molesting or assaulting her (non-molestation order) and gives her the right to remain in the matrimonial home by excluding the violent partner (exclusion order). If the partner breaks the injunction by assaulting the woman or entering the matrimonial home, he can be taken to court for 'contempt'. If a judge has attached powers of arrest for breach of injunction, the police can arrest the man there and then. If the police do not arrest, a woman or her solicitor must take the man back for 'contempt of court'.

It is widely held amongst women in refuges that injunctions are ineffective. Although there may be difficulties obtaining an injunction, the main problem seems to arise in their enforcement. Over all, 35 women in our follow-up study (42%) had obtained an injunction, either before or after leaving their partner. Of these 17 had called the police because of their partners violence. However, only 4 men out of the 17 committing assault were charged with breaking the injunction, although 10 of the women had either nearly been killed or suffered injuries requiring hospitalisation. Even when the men had been charged the punishment was again light, ranging from fines of £20 to £75 to a dressing down in court.

A more common response to domestic violence when women had injunctions was for the police to try and calm down the situation – in other words, to respond in the same way as they dealt with women without injunctions. In 8 out of the 17 calls for help – i.e. nearly half – the police had either taken a placatory role or not come to the scene of the violence.

For injunctions to offer immediate protection, the police must arrest on the spot. Otherwise women must wait until the court hearing – sometimes several weeks – during which time they are left unprotected.

'At first I only got a non-molestation order without powers of arrest. Then he tried to get into my flat – threatened me with a knife and said he'd kill me this time. The police said they couldn't help unless I had a powers of arrest clause.'

However, a power of arrest clause seems to have little effect on whether the violent man will be charged. One out of four men were arrested when women had an injunction without a power of arrest clause, while 23% (3 out of 13) were arrested when women had this clause. Police referrals of battered women to refuges were also comparatively small – only 11% of women had been referred by the police. There is clearly a need for improvement in the service the police offer to battered women.

Housing departments

After protection, the other main need of battered women was for alternative accommodation away from the violent partner. In the past, a third of the women in our study had approached their local Housing Department for assistance. However, 71% had not found the visit useful.

Women reported being told that there was nothing that could be done either immediately or in the long term.

'They said it was up to me to find somewhere.'

'They couldn't do anything about rehousing me while he was in the house.'

'I told them about my husband breaking up the house and they just said I'd have to pay for it.'

Many of these approaches to Housing Departments would have been made before the introduction of the Housing (Homeless Persons) Act 1977, which clarified the obligations of Housing Departments to certain groups of homeless people, including battered women. However, even before the Act, Department of Environment Circular 18/74 had stressed the responsibilities of Housing Departments towards the homeless.

Only 8% of women had been referred to refuges by Housing Departments. There was also a tendency for Departments to put women in bed and breakfast accommodation where they would gain little personal and practical support. Chapter 8 contains a fuller discussion of women's experiences of obtaining permanent housing.

Social services

Social Services had been contacted by over half the women in the national survey, but nearly half of these (48%) had not found the contact useful.* A quarter of the women complained that social workers had tried to reconcile them to their violent partners, or had tried to stop them leaving.

> 'I rang social services because I was so desperate to leave and they said 'all we can do if you leave is we'll take the children off you and take them into care and we don't want that, do we?' So I said 'no' and that was it.'

Others complained that social workers had said there was nothing they could do to help. Women often felt that social workers were not interested. As in the case of the police, there was a general feeling amongst women that their desperate situation was not taken seriously. Off-hand remarks by individual social workers were frequently mentioned.

> 'They said the only way I could get out of my situation was by winning the pools.'

> 'They told me to wait until my husband put me out on the street.'

It was clear from our interviews with battered women that many social workers saw their role as similar to that of the police in cases of domestic violence, i.e. as mediators in the situation, helping to reconcile the couple through counselling. In an attempt to find out in more detail how social workers view their cases of domestic violence, Maynard analysed 103 randomly selected case records written by social workers in 1977, in a northern town.[16] She found that over a third of cases involved domestic violence, frequently very severe. However, in only three cases were the social workers centrally concerned about the battering. Their main concern was the children.

Despite the impact violence was having on these women's lives (seven women had attempted suicide and 10 had spent some time in mental hospital), action taken by social workers on their behalf was as follows: in 10 cases nothing was done, three cases were referred to Marriage Guidance Councils,† one was advised to take a holiday, several social workers had discussed the problem with the woman but rarely with the man and two women had been placed in mental

---

*Jan Pahl's[10] findings from battered women approaching social services showed that the same proportion had not found the contact useful (48%)
†As can be seen from Table 10, Marriage Guidance had been useful to only 33% of women who contacted it.

hospitals after having been battered. Only two women went to the local refuge and they went of their own accord.

Social workers' responses to assaults on women in the home thus varied considerably and depended on the discretion and knowledge of the individual. 52% of women consulting social workers had found them useful, usually because they had offered them some form of practical help, such as referring them to a refuge. In fact, social service departments were by far the largest referral agency to refuges, accounting for 37% of the women in the survey.

Doctors

Fifty two per cent of the women in the survey had contacted their doctor for help with this problem, but 44% of these had not found the contact useful.* Our findings confirm those of Pahl that 'doctors who persisted in treating only the medical aspects, and offering only medical solutions, were more likely to be perceived as being unhelpful'.[10]

A criticism mentioned by one third of those who had not found doctors useful, was that they had only been offered tranquilisers. In the Dobash study,[1] 40% of women interviewed volunteered that they had been given drugs. Elston, Fuller and Murch in their study of battered women seeking divorce found that 16 out of 17 women who went to their doctor were given drugs. They question the use of drugs which result in drowsiness and loss of decision-making ability at a time when women need help in making a decision about their future. Such lack of control, they suggest, could make self-defence even more difficult in the event of further attack. They also question the appropriateness of treating the woman rather than the man.[5]

Several women in our survey volunteered that they had been sent to psychiatrists by their doctors. R & R Dobash[1] suggest that the willingness of women to undergo psychiatric treatment to bring a resolution of the problem is yet one step further in the problem becoming hers rather then his.

Although it has been estimated[1] that 25% of all violent crime is wife assault, doctors have little training in dealing with anything but the external manifestations of the violence. Pressure on surgery time like-wise discourages doctors from enquiring more deeply into patient's personal difficulties. Several women in this study had been discouraged from phoning or visiting the surgery with that particular problem as there was 'nothing they could do'.

*47% of women in J. Pahl's study[10] had not found their doctors useful in this matter.

Generally, it seems that even where doctors were sympathetic.to the women's situation, they were often unaware of the resources now available to battered women. Only 2% of women had been referred to the refuge by their doctor, although 52% of the women in the survey had contacted them for help.

Voluntary agencies

The most useful agencies to battered women were to be found in the voluntary sector – e.g. Women's Aid (80% found it useful), Gingerbread (79%). However, these are relatively unknown and were consulted by far fewer women.

Women's Aid was the agency thought to be useful by most women – 80% of women who had contacted them in the past. By providing both protection from violence in the refuge and accommodation for as long as women need it, Women's Aid is fulfilling the two major immediate needs of battered women. The fact that relatively few women had contacted them for help is partly due to the comparatively recent appearance of refuges. Refuges were often struggling organisations with few resources for publicity. Some groups reported that they had difficulty supporting the present number of women in refuges with inadequate financial resources and were therefore wary of further publicity. Gingerbread, a self-help organisation for single parents had put battered women up in their homes and offered them support and advice.

Voluntary agencies found most useful by battered women were those that were able to inform women of their legal and financial position and/or readily referred women to refuges.

Relatives and friends

Women suffering violence were more likely to have contacted their relatives for help than anyone else, particularly for emergency accommodation, and on the whole they were found useful. Relatives and friends together were one of the biggest sources of referral to refuges. Seventeen per cent of women heard about refuges from friends or relatives. However, families sometimes put pressure on women to return home or had just lost sympathy for them because they had taken their husband back in the past.

Most women had tried both formal and informal sources of help. However, 20% (125 women) had had no contact with friends or relatives over this problem and had been entirely dependent on statutory or voluntary agencies.

Summary

The difficulty battered women had obtaining practical assistance has been shown both by the high number of agencies women had approached in the past and their dissatisfaction with those agencies. In all, only half the consultations to statutory agencies had been found useful by the women in this study. The work of agencies was often unco-ordinated so a woman had to start each application for help from the beginning again, leading to demoralisation and the feeling that her needs were not being taken seriously.

Women's main expectations were that action would be taken against the man for his assault and that she would be given assistance in leaving the man if she asked for it. If women had approached the wrong agency they expected to be directed to the agency that would be able to help. It seemed however that the two agencies most able to fulfill women's needs i.e. the police and Housing Departments – were often failing in the service they provided.

In 1975, the Select Committee on Violence in Marriage recommended that women assaulted in the home should be entitled to the full protection of the law. Evidence from this study and others shows that police arrests were not being made unless the injury was severe and usually not even then. Many women had thus received no protection from the law against their partner's assaults. Injunctions in practice provided neither immediate nor future protection from assault and it was often only when their husbands were in prison that women had peace of mind.

The response to battered women varied not only across agencies but also between individuals within them. Sometimes officials may have been ignorant of the measures that can be taken but there was also a reluctance among many to intervene in what were regarded as private disputes. This tendency of officials to see their role as peace keepers when dealing with domestic violence meant that men were able to beat their wives with impunity.

3. Refuge Provision in England and Wales

The publicity surrounding the use of women's centres as refuges for battered women in the early 1970s led to a concern that women should not be forced to remain in the marital home to suffer serious and persistent violence. Recognition that the needs of battered women were not being met by statutory agencies led to the formation of voluntary groups and the setting up of refuges. Here we describe what refuges are, their growth and present distribution, and the extent to which they are meeting demand.

What are refuges?

The main aim of all refuge groups is the provision of safe, emergency accommodation for battered women and their children. The majority of groups also offer support and information, and help women find long-term accommodation if they decide to leave their violent husband permanently.

Two thirds of the 150 groups running refuges belong to the Women's Aid Federations of England and Wales. Affiliated groups share a common view on the way in which refuges should be run: they accept women into their refuges on the woman's own definition of need and women can stay as long as they need to reorganise their lives. Residents organise the day-to-day running of the house. Mutual self-help is stressed as an important step towards women gaining self-confidence and being able to cope when they leave the refuge. The Women's Aid group is there to provide whatever information and assistance women need, as far as their resources allow. Groups also aim to publicise their work giving talks and presenting exhibitions to increase public awareness of battering.

The growth of refuges and their present distribution

There has been a steady increase in the number of groups running refuges since 1973: by September 1978 there were 150 refuge groups, running approximately 200 houses. Over the period September 1977-78, an estimated 11,400 women and 20,850 children used refuge accommodation in England and Wales. At any one time during the year there were about 900 women and 1,700 children living in refuges. Two years later the numbers accommodated were much the same.

The Select Committee on Violence in Marriage recommended in 1975 that the number of refuges be increased to provide one family place per 10,000 of the population. This would bring the number of refuges up to 982. In September 1978 refuge provision amounted to only one sixth of that level. (See Table 12). While the Select Committee's estimate of need was not based on any firm figures, there is nevertheless much to suggest that present refuge provision is not adequately meeting current expressed demand (i.e. the number of women actually requesting refuge places), let alone hidden demand that might emerge due to greater publicity or the opening of more refuges.

Table 12 : A comparison between existing refuge provision in metropolitan districts and the level of provision recommended by the select committee

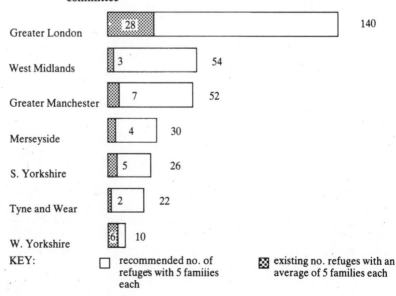

Greater London	28	140
West Midlands	3	54
Greater Manchester	7	52
Merseyside	4	30
S. Yorkshire	5	26
Tyne and Wear	2	22
W. Yorkshire	6	10

KEY: ☐ recommended no. of refuges with 5 families each   ⊠ existing no. refuges with an average of 5 families each

Refuges in England and Wales September 1978

Metropolitan Countries

Greater London:	28
Greater Manchester:	7
Merseyside:	4
W. Yorkshire:	6
S. Yorkshire:	5
West Midlands:	3
Tyne & Wear:	2

● = 1 refuge, not necessarily of 5 places.

Total number of refuges = 150

▨ Metropolitan country

▬▬▬ Standard region boundary

─── County boundary

Figure 1

Firstly refuges are unevely distributed across the country. In 1978 when the survey took place, the highest level of provision in any county reached only a quarter of the recommended level. But most counties had less than a fifth and some less than a tenth of the recommended level. It was not necessarily the large Metropolitan areas which had the highest levels of provision. The West Midlands Metropolitan District, for example, had only 6% of the recommended level and Greater Manchester only 13%. Generally, however, it was the rural areas which were least well-catered for and in these areas provision is more of a problem.* Anonymity is more difficult to maintain and women from such areas may need to travel further away for their own safety.

The emergence of a refuge in a particular area did not necessarily mean that demand was higher there than elsewhere. In general, it was depenent on the co-existence of two factors: both a group of local women intent on setting up a refuge, and the willingness of the local council to co-operate with this aim by providing a property for rent This piecemeal approach has left large areas of the country without refuge provision.

Refuges were not meeting present demand for places. They were usually occupying houses meant for single family occupation, so there were high levels of overcrowding in most refuges. Over half the women interviewed had had to move away from their local authority to find refuge. Although some had moved for safety reasons, insufficient provision in their own areas meant that many women had had to move to a strange town at a time when they would have most valued the support of friends and relatives.

Women from areas with no refuge have little or no possibility of being referred to a refuge elsewhere. Only 72 women (11%) came from areas where there was no refuge provision. It is unlikely that the need for refuge places was actually lower in these areas. More probably, other agencies are referring women to refuges only on a very local basis. Agencies in towns without refuges are either unaware of or not making use of refuges further afield.

So in large areas of the country battered women had no access to refuges at all, while even where refuges did exist, they were failing to meet present demand for places.

---

*see S. Delamont and R. Ellis[9] p.12, p.59-62 for a discussion of refuge provisions in rural areas.

Local Authority involvement in refuges

Eighty three per cent of the properties used as refuges are rented from local authorities. Many authorities see refuge provision as one way in which they can meet their obligations under the homelessness legislation. However, most groups running refuges reported that they had had to campaign long and hard to get properties from the council and many groups were still without any financial support. In September 1978 at least 30 groups were trying to get a property for use as a refuge. The main obstacle was the unwillingness of many local authorities to support such projects.

There are still some councils who do not accept that battering is widespread: they may well take the view that battering is not a problem in their area. This is contrary to the growing body of literature on the subject† and the experience of refuges which generally cannot cope with the demand from battered women in all types of areas.

With the passing of the Housing (Homeless Persons) Act and the Domestic Violence Act, local authorities have sometimes argued that there is now no need for refuges. Women, they say, can use Homeless Families Accommodation or can return to their old home with an exclusion order to keep their husband or boyfriend out. However, homeless families temporary accommodation is not always available and women said it did not provide the protection and help offered by refuges. Also, exclusion orders are usually ineffective in preventing men from returning to the marital home and harassing their wives.*

Despite some local authorities' reluctance to support refuge initiatives, there has been a gradual increase in refuge provision in England and Wales since 1974. However, in that period, of the 202 houses opened by 114 groups, a quarter had been shut down. (See Table 13).

Summary

By 1978 there were 150 groups running an estimated 200 houses in England and Wales but refuge provision had reached only a sixth of the level recommended by the Select Committee on Violence in Marriage in 1975 and was not adequately meeting current demand. In addition, large areas of the country were still without any refuge

†See Introduction
*See Chapter 10.

**Table 13 : Number of refuges opened and closed by 114 groups in England
and Wales 1973-78**

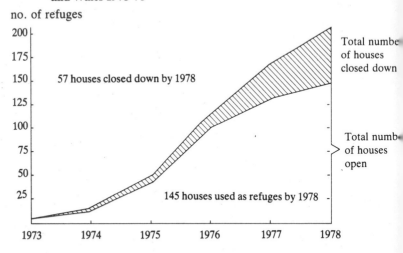

no. of refuges

200 — Total number of houses closed down

57 houses closed down by 1978

145 houses used as refuges by 1978

Total number of houses open

1973   1974   1975   1976   1977   1978

provision and demand in these areas remains unknown, since women
from these areas were seldom referred to refuges elsewhere. While
local authorities supported refuge provision in many areas by providing properties for rent, in many others refuge initiatives had failed
because of lack of local authority support.

4. The Physical Conditions in Existing Refuges

The sort of properties used as refuges

Most groups had had little or no choice in the type or location of properties used as refuges. They varied enormously, from large detached houses with numerous rooms to small terraced houses containing only two or three bedrooms. The condition of the property and the standard of basic amenities likewise varied from house to house. But in the opinion of the groups who responded to the questionnaire it was generally regarded as poor and well below average family accommodation. The houses were usually old – over half were built before 1919 and three quarters before the 2nd World War. A few houses had been newly renovated and redecorated and were in relatively good physical condition. However many others were reported to be in poor structural condition, sited in redevelopment areas and appeared shabby and dilapidated. Many were in fact short life properties on which the local authority were unwilling to spend any further money. The following groups' descriptions illustrate the range of conditions that were found in refuges:

'The house is a small 2 bedroomed terraced house with a downstairs room used as an extra bedroom. The rooms are damp and fairly dingy. We have constant electrical faults. The house is the only one in the street that is lived in as it is a demolition area. It has been broken into by vandals several times and things stolen and twice the phone has been ripped off the wall. There is no play space so the kids use the street which is littered with broken glass.'

'The new premises are superb, and the facilities are much better, i.e. 3 bathrooms, laundry, central heating, large kitchen, 6 bedrooms, 2 sitting rooms, (one will be a dining room), and a very large playroom.'

'Our house is a damp one-bedroomed end terrace in a back street much of which will soon be demolished. There is no play area for the children, a very small kitchen, a dark kitchen diner, hall with peeling paint, bathroom with fungus and faulty electrics, a boxroom used as a bedroom and another bedroom with five beds in it.' (This house was being shared by three women and six children).

Properties were often in old inner-city areas, which did however have some advantages. Three-quarters of the women interviewed thought the refuge was in a good position because of its proximity to shops, schools and the agencies they needed to consult. Where women said the refuge was badly sited, the main criticisms were that it was in a run-down area, often close to a main road, and too easily visible to men looking for them. On the whole, however, women favoured central locations rather than isolated estates.

Overcrowding in refuges

One of the most striking features about refuges was the number of women and children living in them at any one time. Three bed-roomed houses were quite commonly housing six women and 10 or 12 children, although there were only amenities for one family. Bed-rooms were frequently crammed with three sets of bunk beds, cots and the personal belongings of two or three families. The Bedroom Standard of Occupation,† used by local authorities in allocating council property, was exceeded in nearly every refuge. Forty three per cent of women were sharing their bedrooms with other families and 82% shared their bedroom and sometimes even their beds with their own children.

The number of women and children sharing a refuge ranged from one to 36 families, but on average there were six women and nine children per refuge. Yet refuges usually contained one kitchen, one cooker and sink, one bathroom, two toilets and no dining room or laundry room. Some of the larger houses did have more than one of these basic amenities but these houses were usually occupied by at least five and sometimes as many as 15 families.

Some councils tried to control overcrowding in refuges imposing a limit on numbers. However, groups were unwilling to turn women away for fear they would be put off from seeking help again.

---

†Bedroom Standard of Occupation is used in most social survey research to assess levels of overcrowding. See Gray, P.G. and Russell, R: *Housing Situation 1960*. It states that adults should not have to share bedrooms with children and that children of the opposite sex over 10 should not have to share bedrooms.

Number of women and children sharing accommodation

No. of Women Sharing Accommodation		No. of Children Sharing Accommodation	
Houses with under 4 women sharing	23%	Houses with under 6 children sharing	28%
Houses with 4–6 women sharing	34%	Houses with 7–9 children sharing	24%
Houses with 7–9 women sharing	33%	Houses with 10–19 children sharing	40%
Houses with 10+ women sharing	10%	Houses with 20+ children sharing	8%

Some of the 9 women and 22 children living in two adjacent 3-bedroomed houses.

The existence of such high levels of overcrowding indicates the extent to which current refuge provision falls short of demand. It is not known how many women leave refuges without the help they need because of overcrowding.

Lack of amenities

There were seldom enough basic amenities for the numbers of women and children using them. (See Table 14). The areas under most pressure were those essential facilities shared by all the women, i.e. kitchen and cookers, bathroom and toilets, and washing and drying facilities. Three-quarters of the houses had no laundry room and over half had no dining room. Women had to eat meals in the busy kitchen or off their laps in the bedroom or sitting room. Lack of laundry facilities placed added strain on other areas of the house. The difficulty of drying clothes was even more acute in wet weather, when

Table 14 : Type and number of facilities provided in most refuges

	COOKING FACILITIES		
Kitchens	Cookers	Sinks	Fridges
1	1	1	1

	DINING FACILITIES	
Dining Rooms	Dining Tables	Dining Chairs
0	1	4

	BATHROOM AND W.C.		
Bathrooms	Shower	W.C. in bathroom	Sep.W.C.
1	0	1	1

	LAUNDRY FACILITIES		
Laundry	Washing Machines	Spin Driers	Tumble Driers
0	1	0	0

SLEEPING ARRANGEMENTS		
Bedroom	%age sharing bed/m other families	%age sharing bed with own children now or in the past
4	43%	38%

	SITTING ROOM	
Sitting Room	Easy chairs	T.V.s
1	4-8	1

These facilities were shared by on average 6 women and 9 children

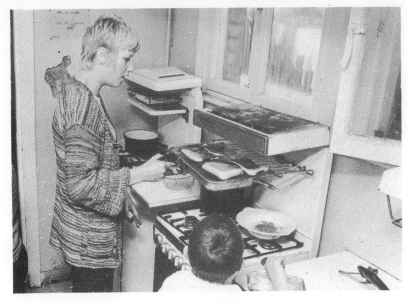

"Cooking breakfast in the morning is like cooking it in middle of Castle Market."

"At tea-time it's like a mad-house in here, all the kids back from school wanting their tea, but there's only one cooker so we all have to take turns."

"There's no dining room here so we just eat where we can."

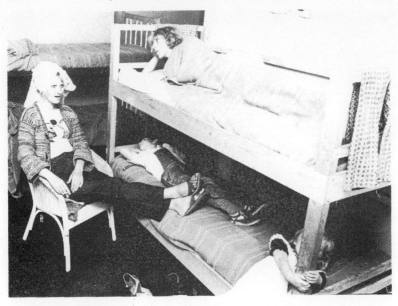

Bunk beds filled up most available space in bedrooms and left no place to hang clothes.

There were 3 women and 4 children sleeping in 4 bunks in this small bedroom: "It's like living in a suitcase."

Women's Aid groups could do little with such poorly maintained
council properties.

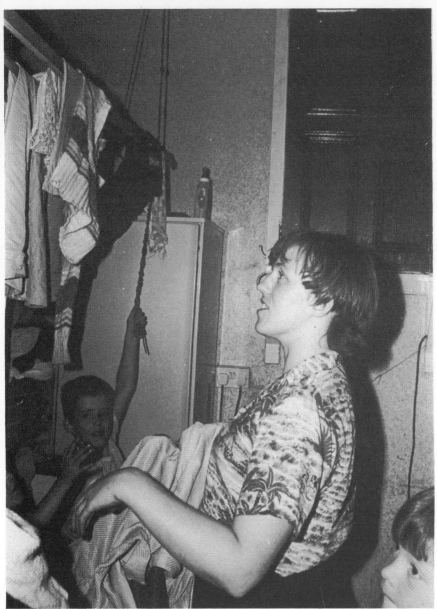

"Come on Mam, it's heavy!" Washing and drying clothes in an already overcrowded kitchen.

Crowded sitting room on a rainy afternoon

washing had to ʰ draped in front of fires or hung around the room.

Even where better facilities did exist, they had to be shared with up to 10 other families. Living in such conditions meant that women had to spend a large part of their day queuing to use the one cooker, sink, bath, toilet and washing machine.

There was also a shortage of essential furniture, such as tables and chairs and other household equipment. Insufficient cupboards, wardrobes and storage space generally meant that women found it hard to keep food safely and hygienically. Personal possessions and clothes were frequently kept in suitcases or bundled in black plastic bags under the beds. It is not surprising that almost all the women criticised the lack of sufficient amenities.

Keeping the refuge warm was a problem for most groups, particularly for those running old houses in a poor state of repair. Expensive or inadequate heating systems meant houses were often cold and draughty. Many groups could not afford to install central heating and so relied on open gas or electric fires which were both uneconomical to run and a potential fire risk with so many children around, as were the overcrowded cooking facilities. One group described the problems they had heating a three bedroomed house:

'Our last quarterly bill was £500 for gas and electricity and that's just for 3 gas fires and an immersion heater. It's very cold in here in winter, so the women leave the gas oven on all the time to heat the kitchen.'

Poor maintenance

The condition of the basic amenities quickly deteriorated due to the continual turnover of users, especially large numbers of children of all ages. In furnishing the refuge, many groups had been totally dependent on appeals to the public and so much of the furniture and household equipment was second-hand and was constantly breaking down. Over half the women were critical of the bad state of repair or the poor decorative condition of the refuge. As a detailed examination of refuge funding shows, (see Chapter 5), many groups had minimal financial resources and were unable to replace and mend broken and worn-out equipment as often as they would have liked. Although most refuges were frequently redecorated and some groups did spend money from fund-raising on repairs, many felt this to be the responsibility of the local authority for whom they were, in effect, providing a service at very little cost.

"We have to decorate the refuge about every six months because so many people live here."

Women's assessment of basic amenities

With such inadequate conditions, the levels of dissatisfaction reported by women were, not suprisingly, very high. In the DOE National Dwelling and Housing Survey (1978) only between 10% and 15% of households were dissatisfied with their accommodation, whereas 30% to 40% of women in our survey were dissatisfied with each amenity. Overall 83% were dissatisfied with at least one of the following facilities: the kitchen and eating facilities, the bedroom and sleeping arrangements, the sitting room, the bathroom and toilets, and washing and drying facilities.

Table 15 : Dissatisfaction in relation to numbers in refuge

44% of women	fewer than 4 families in refuge

54% of women	4-6 families in refuge

61% of women	7 more families in refuge

Total: 636 women

There is little doubt that women's dissatisfaction reflected the actual conditions in refuges. Generally the women's and group's descriptions corresponded closely and were echoed by the interviewers. Where women were most dissatisfied, they were most likely to be living in overcrowded conditions with few facilities,* for example, with no dining room or only one bathroom.

Refuge design

For most women coming to a refuge was their first experience of communal living. Despite the lack of privacy and bad conditions many had found the experience a positive one. Women were asked whether they would prefer refuges to have completely self-contained units or some communal facilities – two-thirds of the women were in favour of the latter, half of whom wanted their own bathroom facilities.

---

*Women's dissatisfaction did not vary with either their length of stay in the refuge, or with their age, number of children or their previous tenure. Social factors such as the deterioration of women's mental health, or their dislike of the way the refuge was run cannot account for the high levels of dissatisfaction, since although related to dissatisfaction they affected less than a third of the women.

Table 16 : How women would prefer refuges to be designed

Design Preferred	No. of women	%age of women
Communally but in good condition	216	34%
Own bedroom, bathroom but with communal living space	191	30%
Completely self-contained flats in the same block or house	229	36%
Total	636	100%

Living communally enabled women to share housework, babysitting and sometimes even cooking. Women found many advantages in living with others (see Chapter 6).

'We used to have a laugh – sit up every night till 2 o'clock, talking. We used to help each other, baby-sit for each other. It felt like my own home.'

However just over a third of the women would have preferred completely self-contained units in the same block/house as other battered women, but many of these women would have preferred not to have come through a refuge at all.

'I find with young children that if the baby wakes up, it wakes the other children up and I'm a wreck in the morning. I have to sleep with six children in the room. I don't like having to share the kitchen, bathroom and toilet. If we have to share the kitchen and bathroom there should be just two families at the most. It would be nice to have separate flats in one house.'

The sort of accommodation that would seem to gain majority support from women in our survey, would be a mixture of self-contained amenities, i.e. own bedroom with separate room for the children and a communal living room, playroom and laundry, with kitchens and bathrooms shared by two to three families at the most.

Summary

A detailed examination of existing refuges reveals that much of the property was unsuitable. Although some refuges were in good physical condition, it was more common to find sub-standard property, which was old and in a poor structural state. Half the groups felt the council did not maintain the property adequately and lack of funds for groups running refuges resulted in insufficient and often broken amenities. Great stress was placed on women living in the refuges by the high levels of overcrowding, and generally the demand for refuge places far exceeded the present number. As a result the majority of women were highly dissatisfied with the physical conditions, but they were prepared to put up with them chiefly because there was nowhere else to go.

5. The Funding Of Refuges

Group's incomes

The total income of refuge groups for the year September 1977-78, ranged from £296 to £35,986, out of which all running costs had to be met. Half the groups had an income of £5,000 or less. The range of groups' incomes is shown below:

Table 17 : The range of groups' incomes for 1978

Income	No. groups	%age
Less than £2,500	21	24%
£2,500–£4,999	21	24%
£5,000 – £14,999	25	28%
£15,000 or more	21	24%
Total	88*	100%

The chief ways in which income was raised, were rent from residents, fund raising, and most importantly, grants. Access to grant funding varied across the country and from group to group: the Midlands, Yorkshire and the South West were the poorest regions, with groups having an average income less than £5,000 per annum in each of these. Groups in some other regions had an average income of double or in one case, treble that amount. In four regions, 70% of the groups received no grants at all. London groups were the most well off, with an average income of £17,433 per annum, but even here it was possible to find groups with a very low income.

*Only 88 out of 114 groups gave full financial details.

Sources of funding

Groups received funding from a variety of sources (see Table 18), all of it temporary, although some sources of funding were more secure and the size of their grants considerably bigger, than others. The biggest single source of funds was the Urban Aid Programme, accounting for a third of total grant funding. The grants were larger than those from other sources and they were more secure, lasting up to 5 years. The Manpower Services Commission was the other important source of funding, covering 26% of grant funding, but the money was only for one year at a time. There were a few much smaller grants from Social Service Departments, Housing Departments and Trusts.

Table 18 : Sources of grant funding for 1978 and 1980

Source	Average Amount.	No. Groups Rec.	%age Groups Rec.	
1978				
Urban Aid	£7,220	28	25%	Total 88 groups
Social Services	£3,063	29	25%	surveyed
Trusts	£1,825	24	21%	
M.S.C.	£8,609	20	18%	
Housing Depts.	£785	10	9%	
1980				
Urban Aid	£10,940	29	35%	Total = 83
Social Services	£4,373	13	16%	groups surveyed
Local Council	£2,602	11	14%	
Housing Depts.	£4,089	10	12%	
Trusts	£4,300	2	2%	
M.S.C.	£5,928	1	1%	

In 1978, then, Women's Aid groups had little access to secure funding. Thirty nine per cent of groups received no grants at all. Those who did mostly received small amounts and were providing an extremely cheap service. Most felt that they needed better funding to run effectively. In order to assess whether groups' financial position had improved or deteriorated over the 2 years, we sent a brief questionnaire in 1980 to all groups which had participated in the original survey. Eighty three were returned: their sources of funding can be seen in Table 18 above.

What emerges, is that there has been little improvement in refuge funding and in fact, existing sources of funding are disappearing or under threat. Six groups had closed in the last year, due to lack of funds or council refusal to renew their lease. A further six faced imminent closure.

The proportion of groups receiving more than £1,000 in grant funding had increased by 10%, but the average amount received had only just kept pace with inflation,† and was still very low indeed. In real terms, groups were suffering, for example, funded groups could afford only 57 hrs. of paid work a week, compared to the 84 hrs. per week they had in 1978.

The Manpower Services Commission had virtually disappeared as a source of funding for refuges, only one group still receiving it. This has had a crippling effect on many groups. For some it had been their whole source of funding for several years and now they were totally dependent on voluntary labour. One East Anglian group had lost five full-time workers when their M.S.C. grant expired, without being able to find any other source of funding. Another group in a similar position said:

> 'We teeter permanently on the brink of closure because of lack of money and volunteers.'

In a few cases, the loss of M.S.C. funding had been partly compensated for by local authority funding, but, whereas groups had received on average £8,606 from M.S.C. in 1978, they were receiving on average only £2,607 from local and district councils and £4,089 from Housing Departments in 1980. Despite its disadvantages, groups had suffered a severe financial loss when M.S.C. funding expired.

Urban Aid had by 1980 become the chief and almost sole source of funding for refuges, accounting for 68% of the total income of groups. Although there had been an increase in the proportion of groups receiving it between 1978 and 1980, over half the groups now benefitting from Urban Aid were due to lose this source of funding by April 1981. It may prove to be the case that refuges reapplying for this form of funding will stand a good chance of success. Nevertheless, Urban Aid cannot be regarded as a permanent source of funding for refuges. This, taken together with the cessation of M.S.C. funding could have disastrous consequences on both the level and quality of refuge provision.

Then there are the groups who have not had access to Urban Aid,

†To make an exact comparison, we considered only the 53 groups for which we had full financial details for both 1978 and 1980. The proportion of these receiving grants increased from 53% to 62%, but the average amount received increased from only £4,311 to £5,889.

either because the group was not in an area designated as being 'in special need' or because the local authority did not back their application.

The only other source of funding was direct from local authorities. This could come from Housing Departments under Section 13 of the Housing (Homeless Persons) Act, which gives broad powers to central and local government to make grants and/or loans to voluntary organisations concerned with homelessness. The number of groups benefitting from Section 13 funding has increased very little since 1978, although the amount they received from Housing Departments had increased from an average of £785 to £4,089 per annum. While groups appreciated the fact that cuts in public expenditure had reduced local authority revenue, they felt it was nevertheless in councils interest to provide financial support for refuges, since they were enabling councils to fulfil their duties under the Housing (Homeless Persons) Act and very cheaply, at that.

The effects of grant funding

In 1978, as many as 39% of groups received grants totalling £1,000 or less for a year – called 'unfunded' groups. These grants were usually from trusts and social services departments. Their average income was only £2,980, less than a quarter of that of the funded groups. Most of it was spent on rent, repairs and bills for heating, lighting and telephone. Lack of funding seriously curtailed the work these groups could do. In the previous year, they had been able to put up only half the number of women that the funded groups had housed and they had been able to spend less than a third of the amount on repairs. Running a refuge is a time-consuming business, and without money for paid workers, some of these groups found themselves in a vicious circle, having little time to fund-raise or attract new members without distracting from their work in the refuge.

Even where groups were funded by external bodies, their incomes were still comparatively low. The average income of funded groups was £13,004 with a fair proportion of it still being raised from fund-drives and rent from residents. Because of the poor properties they usually occupied, these groups were having to spend a quarter of their income, once salaries were deducted, on repairs. Both funded and unfunded groups were paying high rents – the average rent paid was £824 a year, and almost a third of groups paid more than £1,000. In only a few cases did local authorities assist groups by agreeing to a nominal rent.

The bulk of money received from grants was specifically to cover salaries for paid workers. However, funded groups were able to spend more money on all other areas of expenditure as well – for example, transport, rent and furnishing.

The paid work groups could? afford ranged from one part-time worker to as many as four or five full-time workers in a few cases. On average, groups with funding could afford 84 hrs. of paid work a week in their refuges. About 60% of this time was spent on 'general refuge work' – which included help and information on housing and other rights, liaising with agencies and generally ensuring the smooth running of the refuge. A further 20% of paid work time was spent specifically on children and the remainder taken up by a variety of jobs, such as organisers, wardens, publicity and follow-up workers. In all, 60 groups (53%) said they needed more money for paid work; of the 105 extra workers they wanted between them, most were for general refuge work and for work with children.

Summary

At the time of the survey, most groups were poorly funded and this has not improved. Groups were often finding it difficult to maintain their services, let alone to expand them or to improve the conditions in refuges. Some groups have since had to close down because of lack of funds, others have had to make workers redundant. What sources there were, Manpower Services Commission and Urban Aid, were not secure and have begun to dry up. The only realistic source of funding, local authorities, has not taken over from the temporary sources as Women's Aid groups had hoped.

6. What Refuges Offer Battered Women

Refuges differ from other types of emergency accommodation in that they aim to meet a wide range of needs women have when escaping from violent men. Women needed safe accommodation and also help, information and support in reorganising their lives. Solicitors had to be consulted, social security or maintenance arranged and permanent housing applied for. In this chapter we look at the sort of help offered and the experience of living in a refuge. Most women valued their stay in a refuge and felt that without the range of help they had received, they would not have been able to make a permanent break.

Protection

Protection was one of the main needs of battered women seeking help. Most of the women interviewed were terrified of being found by their violent partners; 'He'd kill me if he found me' we were often told. The experience of Women's Aid groups showed that these fears were not exaggerated – in extreme cases women had been murdered. More often, men harassed women by, for example, hanging around outside the refuge or phoning up at all times of the day and night:

> 'He used to phone up the refuge "How's her head? I'll give her a fractured skull next time I see her".'

Occasionally men had broken into the refuge by force and terrorised those inside:

> 'He got into the refuge when he knew I was there. He'd got a gun on him and threatened to murder me. The police were on the roof with binoculars but he still got away. I stayed with a committee member for three months because he was such a nuisance. In the end they had to transfer everyone in the refuge because he still bothered them.'

Plastic glass was installed in the lower windows after yet another break-in by an angry husband. It cost £150.

Another woman was frightened of using the washing line in case her husband recognised her washing if he walked past. Other mothers would not let their children play outside the house in case they were seen from the road. Thus ensuring protection for women and children living in refuges was a primary concern for all groups.

Most Women's Aid groups tried as far as possible to keep their address secret. Within the house strict measures were taken to make the house physically secure. Doors and windows were kept locked and where groups could afford it, reinforced glass in ground floor windows had been installed. It was usual for everyone to identify themselves before the door was opened.

Generally these security measures did deter men and four fifths of women in refuges said they felt safe. Where they did not, it appeared that the police were far more willing to take action than they were in cases of domestic dispute in a private home. While only a third of women found the police helpful before they came to a refuge, three quarters of the groups reported the police were helpful in protecting the refuge. However, the most important source of protection was simply having other people about – this gave women a great sense of security:

'Homeless (Families Accommodation) to battered women is no use anyway. It may be alright after a month or two depending on the sort of person that you are, but for me one of the main things was the safety of the refuge. You knew that if their father did come I had other women there and I had people that would help me.'

Feeling safe was mainly dependent on whether women had kept their whereabouts secret. However, 35% of the women in the survey had already been found by their violent partner. The majority of men did not need to use much ingenuity to discover where their wives or girlfriends were staying. There were numerous ways men found where the refuge was, often through lack of care on behalf of agencies.

Overall 19% of women had had their address revealed through legal proceedings. Divorce and custody petitions and even ironically injunctions, frequently had the address of the women on them, or it was disclosed through court proceedings. Finding the location of the refuge through the children was another main source of discovery (19%). Men followed children back from school or after having access. Women rarely had their own transport, so children walking home were easily followed. The secret address of 9% of the women was lost because of dealings with the social services or social security. Agencies contacting men about maintenance often gave away what town, borough or even what actual address the woman was living at. It was clear that the threat of violence and the danger women were in was frequently underestimated.

There were two courses of action open to women in refuges who were being harassed by their violent partners. They could either attempt to obtain protection through the Domestic Violence Act, or they could move to another town. However emergency injunctions were sometimes difficult to obtain and were not always effective.† Women were, therefore, often forced to flee to another refuge. Almost half the women interviewed were either already living in a different town or would have felt safer in one.

The national network of Women's Aid refuges enabled women to move away where necessary. But this could result in many practical problems, particularly with rehousing.† It was also unsettling to move children to yet another temporary home. Some women found the support of friends, relatives, or the refuge a source of greater strength in warding off angry husbands than the potential safety offered by a distant refuge.

†See Chapter 10 for details on the effectiveness of the Domestic Violence Act.
*See Chapter 8.

Trying to get an emergency payment from Social Security – it paid to take someone experienced with you.

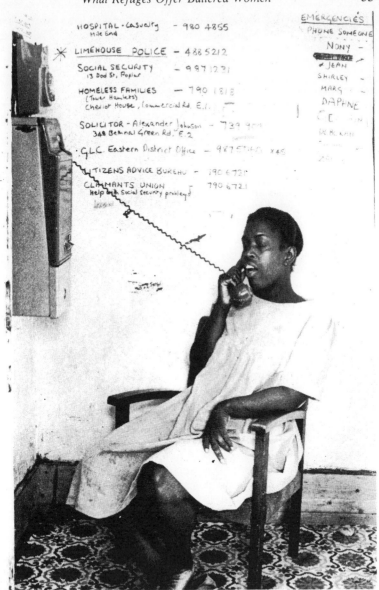

Women were constantly on the phone trying to find out what had happened to their applications for divorce, custody and housing: "You spend all your money just hanging on."

On the other hand where women had stayed in their home town there was obviously a greater risk of being discovered. The reason most women gave for not moving was because they did not know of the existence of refuges elsewhere.

Information

Arriving at a refuge, sometimes in a strange town, women were confronted with a range of practical problems:

> 'It's a lot better for a woman who's nerve-wracked to come through a refuge such as this before she goes any further, because even her solicitor can knock her around with things that she shouldn't pay for and is paying for. The housing's always a good thing to know about too, cos a lot of people aren't told they can get rehoused. It's in a refuge like this that they get to know all these kinds of things. It's quite an eye-opener.'

Most groups assisted women with their claims for social security, applications to housing agencies, and with legal proceedings such as divorce, custody petitions and injunctions.

With such help and information freely available, women were in a better position to make plans for their future. Assistance from the groups ranged from providing the address or phone number of the particular agency the women needed to see, to accompanying the women to the appropriate office or where necessary to the court. Women often experience difficulty in their attempts to obtain social security payments and organise housing and legal matters. Groups then frequently contacted and lobbied the particular agency on women's behalf.

The experience of living in a refuge

Most women arrived at a refuge in a confused and desperate state. The need for company* and understanding from other women was possibly their most immediate need – a chance to talk about their experiences in an atmosphere of sympathy rather than embarrassment:

> 'I used to be ashamed to talk about battering to people. I can really talk openly here because they've all been through the same thing.'

> 'When I first left home, it happened in the night, and when I went to the police they put me in Homeless (Accommodation) for the night. Of course I had an eye out here and I had marks round my neck. The people

---

*Fifty five per cent volunteered that they liked having the company of the other women in the refuge.

"It's so nice to have so many people to talk to and tell your problems to because I've never had anyone before. My husband didn't like me to have girlfriends."

A birthday celebration in the refuge. Children come downstairs to make sure they're not missing anything.

At last, an offer of a house.

there were looking at me and we were like two fugitives there, hid away in our rooms. You know you want to cry, you want to . . . you don't really know what's the matter with you, everything's so bad. If you go into a refuge you know that them other women that's in there have had it too, have gone through it too, so you don't feel so bad and you can let out your feelings 'cos you know that those people understand. They know exactly what you've gone through.'

Many women had suffered violence for years and were left with little self-confidence. The company of other women was particularly valuable to those who had been kept in enforced isolation by their husbands, such as women whose husbands had only allowed them out of the house to do the shopping.

There were definitely advantages for women with similar problems living together:

'All the people there have the same problem, people were so friendly and the workers so good. The other women helped to look after my kids when I had to go into hospital. When I was living at home I hadn't thought much about other people, so meeting other people with similar problems was good. It calmed me down and helped me to be more independent. The workers do what they can but you have to do some things for yourself, so you learn how do do things.'

The progress of each woman's attempts to be rehoused, obtain custody or divorce, helped show new arrivals how they could reorganise their own lives. Worry and confusion about legal proceedings and housing difficulties could be talked over together:

'After two or three days when you've been there and you see another woman come in you try to help her, like you've been helped. You can fit in and discuss things and you know that you're not the only person in the world that's been battered, or even gone through a bad time and it sort of helps you in that way. For that time (in the refuge) you're one of a kind, knowing that you're not on your own is great.'

Developing self-help was an important part of the work of many groups, particularly those affiliated to W.A.F. Women were encouraged to deal with statutory agencies themselves so as to gain experience at it. Many women said they had not been able to before:

'I had to take people on trust, which has been wrong for me all my life – somebody's steam rollered over me. But now I can read and write a bit and I'm fighting – I'm really fighting for my life this time, you know, I'm fighting for my kids. The refuge has been the makings of me.'

Seventy per cent of women said they were involved in the running of the refuge and half went to meetings held by the group:

'We all run it as a group, so we all take decisions.It's like a small community – we all help each other.'

Living in the refuge had often improved women's mental health made them feel stronger and more self-confident:

'I'm going back to how I used to be – happy and carefree. It's been the change of me, the change of the children, my health's got better, so has theirs. I can control them now, I couldn't before. They saw him hit me so they did it too.'

Generally women said that they had gained from the experience of living in a refuge and volunteered far more features of refuge life that they liked than they disliked. The degree to which refuges were providing a supportive environment for battered women can, to some extent, be seen by the improvements women reported in their mental and physical health since being in the refuge.

Despite the problems of overcrowding, over a third of the women reported improvements in their physical health since coming to the refuge. This was often due to women eating and sleeping better. Women felt their appetites had increased and they could also often afford to buy more and better food:

Table 19 : Reported changes in women's mental and physical health

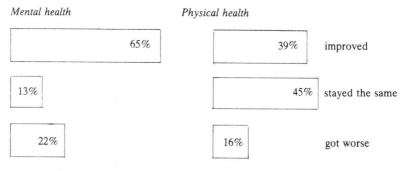

Mental health   *Physical health*

65%	39%	improved
13%	45%	stayed the same
22%	16%	got worse

Total=636 women

'When I came here I was really skinny, and now I've found I've put on a hell of a lot of weight. My husband always wanted steak and chips every day so me and the kids had to make do with what was left. Now I have my own pocket money in my pocket and that's a big achievement.'

The most frequent reason given for liking the refuge was that women said they felt more relaxed than they had before.* They were no longer jumping up anxiously at the sound of the door opening, no longer 'a bag of nerves'. 'I can stand up straight instead of creeping around' said one woman, while another said, 'I don't cry and shake all the time now'. Having got away from the violence, and feeling safe from further threats of violence, was obviously a great relief to many women; 'I couldn't have coped on my own with the threat of violence'.

Complaints about the refuge chiefly focused on the bad physical conditions and overcrowding. Women also found the number of children and the constant noise they made to be one of the hardest aspects of refuge life to cope with (40% mentioned this as a problem).

> 'The kids don't mean it but they bang – up and down the stairs. For the last couple of nights I haven't been able to get the baby to sleep . . . She's getting on my nerves. The kids used to go to bed at 6.00 p.m. and then the other kids say "I don't go to bed until 11" or something like that and it all breaks down.'

Another major dislike was the lack of privacy. Nearly half the women shared a bedroom with another family or families as well as their own children, which meant there was nowhere in the refuge they could go for peace and quiet:

> 'In a place like this you can't lock your door and if you're fed up – I mean I've got a bolt on the inside and outside but you still get the 'knock knock, are you in, are you in?.' I've got nowhere to invite people to – they just come for a couple of hours and go away with a headache.'

Length of refuge stay

The length of time women wanted to stay in the refuge varied. Some women found it difficult to adapt to refuge life and left within a few days. Others, however, stayed for months and felt they had changed dramatically while they were there. Given the advantages and disadvantages of refuge life, women felt that a stay of two months was the ideal length of time. On average three to four months was stated as the longest time they should have to stay in a refuge. However tracing 411 women a year after we had first interviewed them, we found that women had spent anything from one week to three years in a refuge. On average women stayed 5½ months, because of the difficulty of securing long-term accommodation.

*Fifty nine per cent volunteered that they were more relaxed in the refuge.

Table 20 : Total length of time women lived in refuge accommodation†

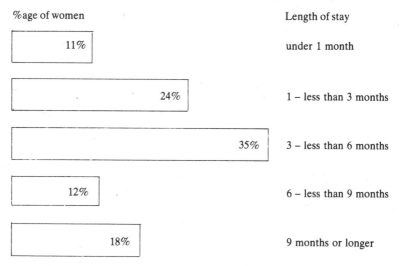

%age of women	Length of stay
11%	under 1 month
24%	1 – less than 3 months
35%	3 – less than 6 months
12%	6 – less than 9 months
18%	9 months or longer

Refuges were set up to provide emergency accommodation. Neither women nor groups felt that they were suitable for long term stays and yet just under a third of the women had been in the refuge for at least six months while 10% were living in refuge accommodation for more than a year. The effect of such long stays was summed up by one woman:

'You get awfully depressed when you see everyone else with a house and you're still here. You have to keep making new friends and they go away and you have to start again. You crack up after six months.'

Another woman, whose application for rehousing had been initially refused, waited in the refuge for five months:

'I mean I was stuck in there not knowing what was going to happen. If I'd known from the beginning I was going to get somewhere I would have been alright, but with the council saying they weren't going to give me anywhere I didn't know what was going to happen. I could just see myself being stuck there forever.'

Women were also worried that staying in the refuge for a long time would make it more difficult for them to cope on their own, once they were rehoused.

'It was a very frightening experience in one way when I did get the house, 'cos I knew that I would be left completely on my own – that was the end of the line with the women not there anymore. Would anybody help me to

†Figures based on information on 411 women one year after being interviewed.

cope with different things? In a way it was great but in another way it was terrifying – would I like living on my own, completely on my own.'

Looking back on their life in the refuge

The 84 women in the follow-up study were asked about their likes and dislikes of refuge life. On the whole women's views of the refuge had changed very little over the 18 months. They still valued the times they had spent in the refuge, especially the companionship of the refuge and the friends they had made there. Overcrowding and bad physical conditions were remembered as being the worst aspects of refuge life.

In retrospect over half of the women said they had changed for the better while in the refuge and now felt stronger and more independent:

'I'm much more determined, manage my money better. Now I want to go back to work.'

'It was safe and I seemed to build up courage when I was there that I'd had knocked out of me. I could stand up to him whereas before I just cowered. I definitely got more courage.'

Almost a third said they thought they had changed for the worse. Their reasons were either the specific conditions in the refuge, such as overcrowding and noise, or the general problems of leaving a relationship and becoming a single parent.

Table 21 : Whether women wanted to come to a refuge or not

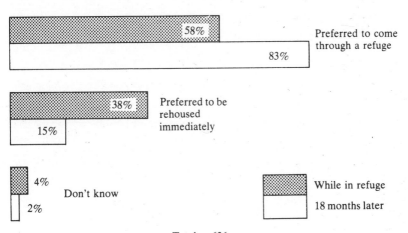

58% / 83% — Preferred to come through a refuge

38% / 15% — Preferred to be rehoused immediately

4% / 2% — Don't know

While in refuge / 18 months later

Total = 636

The extent to which women valued the refuge can be seen from the large increase in the number of women who said that looking back they were pleased to have come through a refuge rather than being rehoused immediately.

It is also interesting to note that when women in the follow-up survey were asked about who they saw most often, half included someone they had known from the refuge.

Table 22 : People women saw most often

	No. of women	%age
Friends	39	56%
Someone they knew from the refuge	36	51%
Relatives	30	43%
Neighbours	25	36%
Others	17	24%

70 women gave up to 3 people each

Summary

Overall, then, refuges were seen to be a useful source of information, protection and personal support. Three quarters of the women felt they had had enough help from the refuge. Only half of those with social workers (40%) had had enough help from them. It appeared that the constant involvement and help of other residents and Women's Aid groups made for a more continuous and wide-ranging support system than can be achieved by visiting social workers.

Many women felt that without the support of the refuge they would not have been able to make the break: 'I couldn't have done it if I'd been rehoused straight away. I'd probably still be married'. One woman summed up the feelings of many when she said:

'I'm not quite settled yet but as soon as I am I'm going to join Women's Aid. It's a wonderful thing, I don't care what anyone says, I don't know where people like me would be but for refuges, honestly I don't. I mean I put up with it for so many years and took terrible hidings because you don't want to tell people . . . Before I knew anything about Women's Aid time and again I went home and took more until I found there were refuges and places that I could go.'

7. Children in Refuges

Perhaps the most striking feature of refuge life was the pressure of so many children in each refuge. In this chapter we look at facilities for children in refuges and the effects on children of their refuge stay. Lack of space for children's activities and lack of funding for play equipment, meant that facilities for children in refuges were usually either poor or non-existent. Women were more critical of the lack of facilities for children than they were of any other amenities in the refuge. They also found living with so many children in such a confined space one of the hardest aspects of refuge life to cope with. Lack of play facilities therefore affected both children and their mothers. However, mother's reports showed that children were more often than not happier living in the refuge than they had been in the often tense atmosphere of home.

Our survey shows that in the year September 1977-78, 20,850 children were put up in refuges in England and Wales.† Also that there were approximately 1,700 children living in refuge accommodation at any one time during the year.

The 656 women in refuges who were interviewed in the survey, had 1,465 children aged 16 or under. Most (80%) of these children lived with their mother in the refuge.*

There were 9 children per refuge, on average, and 15 or more in a quarter of refuges.

The age of the 1,162 children living in the refuges was as follows:

---

†One hundred and fourteen groups accommodated 15,846 children over the year September 1977-78. The number accommodated in 150 refuges is estimated from this.
*See Tables 1 and 2 in Appendix B for details on where children were living while their mother was in the refuge, and their custody position.

Table 23 : The ages of children in refuges

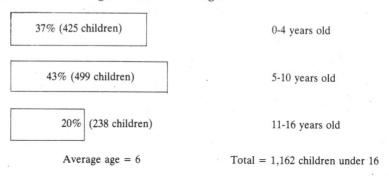

37% (425 children)	0-4 years old
43% (499 children)	5-10 years old
20% (238 children)	11-16 years old
Average age = 6	Total = 1,162 children under 16

Play areas for children in refuges
Inside the refuge

Although children made up nearly two thirds of the refuge population, there was little indoor space allocated specially for children. There was no playroom at all in over half (56%) of the refuges. This meant that the children were all over the house, particularly in busy areas like the kitchen and sitting room. With so many children in each refuge, the noise level was very high and was the feature of refuge life women most disliked.* On wet days – which in most parts of England and Wales make up about a third of the year – children *had* to be indoors and it was at times like these that the need for some playroom/s was most acute. Most children had arrived without their toys and games and generally refuges were poorly supplied with their own. Second-hand toys were frequently at the end of their life when they were donated, and heavy use by large numbers of children meant that most toys were quickly broken or lost.

Even where there were playrooms, half the women interviewed complained that there was often little for children to do in them. They were ofen littered with bits of toys or were being used as temporary storerooms for furniture. To keep paints, paper or other creative play materials in order requires some sort of supervised routine, with materials out of reach when not in use. However, with only a quarter of refuges employing playleaders, work with children and the upkeep of the playroom was generally erratic and depended on the spare time and enthusiasm of voluntary helpers.

*40% of women volunteered that the number of children and the noise they made was the feature they disliked most about refuges.

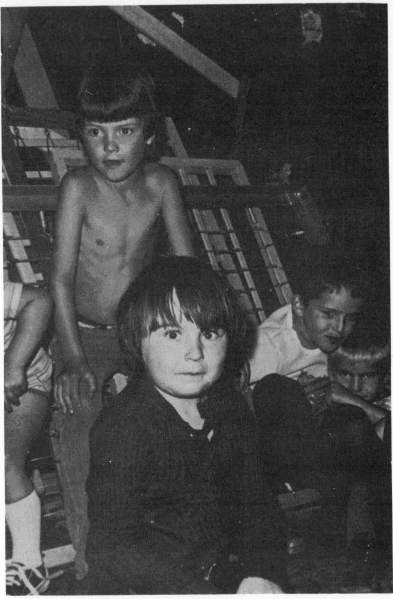

Playrooms are the first to go when space is short. This one is now used as a furniture store.

Some of the lucky few – a creative play environment for children in this refuge.

Outdoors

It is now generally accepted that gardens or some sort of safe outdoor play areas are essential for families with children. With the high numbers of children in each refuge, a garden becomes an absolute necessity. However, some refuges had no outdoor space at all and in many others it consisted of nothing but a small concrete yard with dust-bins and washing lines in it. Women's main complaints were that the garden was too small, not safe from the road and had little for children to do in it.

Dust-bins and broken household equipment often cluttered up the yard or garden for weeks or even months before being removed by council cleansing departments. Not only was this a health risk to children playing outside but the children we interviewed did not like playing in these surroundings. They would have preferred a 'proper garden with flowers and trees, swings and slides'.

The continuing popularity of conventional play equipment[18] suggests that gardens of refuges could be made far more enjoyable places for children by the relatively cheap addition of swings and slides.

Activities arranged for children in refuges

Over a third of children in refuges at the time of the survey were under five. Arrangements for this age-group were probably most crucial as older children were at school for much of the day. However, 44% of groups said that there was nothing arranged for this age-group, either inside or outside the refuge. Not suprisingly, over half the women felt that facilities for this age-group were poor, and were particularly critical of the lack of play equipment available.

Children aged 5–11 seemed to benefit most from the company of their peers in the refuge. However, they were bounding with energy and most women described the after-school period as the most chaotic and difficult to cope with. As the study of children's play activities described in 'Children at Play' showed: the peak ages for active play for both sexes were from 5 to 10.[18] Again, 41% of groups organised nothing at all for this age group inside or outside the refuge.

The funding of activities for children

The amount of money spent on children's play facilities was particularly small – on average 25p per week per child.† Forty one

†Total funds on both salaries for playleaders and play facilities, e.g. play materials, outings and toys, was £88,207 for the year previous to September 1978. In this same period 15,846 children had stayed in these refuges for an average of five months each.

A grim backyard. The donation of a climbing frame made all the difference.

groups (36%) had spent nothing at all on play facilities for children in their refuges over the past year, and half of all groups had spent less than £44 over the same period. The difficulty so many groups had paying rent and major repair bills explains why so little money was spent on children's amenities. Only 44 playleaders were employed by 114 groups in 1978. As some of these were part-time workers in the same refuge, only one quarter of refuges overall had any paid help with children.

As most women (87%) received social security for themselves and their children while in the refuge, women were unable to pay for play materials, new toys and outings to cinemas or fun-fairs. Children in refuges were therefore particularly impoverished as neither the Women's Aid groups nor the children's mothers could afford to provide even the basic toys and play materials they may have had at home.

The need for organised play

Children of all ages benefit from organised play. The DOE design Bulletin 'Children at Play'[18] recommends organised play on the following grounds:

'Supervised play introduces some children to a whole new range of activities, such as opportunities to paint and draw, play with clay, pastry and water, read, play with animals – some of the things which experts agree are so important for the child's healthy development, and essential for learning.'

In refuges organised play became even more necessary. The everyday problems of bringing up children were accentuated. The sheer numbers of children made it impossible to carry out the usual routine of child-care.

Women sometimes arrived in the refuge in a distressed state and were unable to devote much attention to their children. Visiting social security and housing departments often involved long journeys and hours of waiting and were made much more difficult with several young children in tow. Some women had suffered severe violence before coming to the refuge and needed help with child-care while they recovered their physical and mental energy. However, providing organised play in refuges was fraught with problems. Where there were no play-workers activities for children had to be organised by refuge workers or volunteers or not at all. Where there was no play-room it was almost impossible to organise anything for children inside the refuge. Lack of funds restricted all types of activities and lack of transport ruled out most outings any distance from the refuge.

Also, the ages of children in refuges vary tremendously. One week the need will be to provide play facilities for the under-fives and a week later, the children will all be over 8. Any organised play has therefore to be extremely flexible. The needs of children under-five and of children from 5 to 11 are described separately below.

Playgroups

Less than a third of the refuge groups (32%) managed to organise a play-group in the refuge. Where there was a playleader, the hours a playgroup ran were increased from 14 to 22 hours per week on average. The children's enthusiasm for such a playgroup was expressed by Tina:

'I like it when I get up in the morning and I know we're going out or when we stay in and they open the cupboards and we do painting and lots of other things. But once they (workers) go, all the children are bored because they lock up things.'

Almost all women living in refuges with no playgroup would have liked one to be organised – on average 4½ hours a day, either afternoons, or evenings after school. Nearly a quarter, however, would have preferred a playgroup all day.

One of the problems of trying to organise a playgroup in a refuge is that children are moving in and out so frequently. The average length of stay for families was 5½ months, but some children came and went within a fortnight, which meant that any playgroup was very unstable.

For these reasons, using a local playgroup or nursery may be preferable to having a playgroup on the premises. It gives the women a break from having so many children in the house and a relief from the noise. Sixty per cent of groups reported that they had arrangements with local nurseries to take children from the refuge, but only 20% of children under five were attending them. There were several reasons for this: sometimes the playgroups or nursery had a waiting list and the children had just been accepted when they left the refuge again; some playgroups were too far away while others were too expensive; some mothers were reluctant to part with their children fearing it would unsettle them further, and others felt too confused and unsettled themselves to ensure the regular attendance of their children.

It seems to be the case that this particular group of children were failing to use the facilities that did exist in the community precisely because their lives had been disrupted. And it is at times like these when supervised play would have been most valuable.

"I like painting and drawing but they only unlock the playroom twice a week."

The need then, for this age group, is a variety of provision both inside and outside the refuge. Regular attendance at a local play-group and the swift acceptance of new arrivals could be the responsibility of play-workers who could also ensure that women who preferred to have their children with them were assisted during the day in the refuge.

Children from 5 – 11

For this age group the need for organised play was most apparent after they came home from school until about 7 p.m. and also at weekends, which women frequently described as 'murder'. After school children would be running in and out of the kitchen while women were preparing tea. At weekends children would often have nothing to do but race around the refuge banging doors and shouting or arguing about which television channel to watch.

High spirits in the backyard

Play activities for this age group were needed to relieve the pressure on the rest of the occupants. Also to ensure that children's needs were not ignored in the bustle of refuge life. In the 25% of refuges where there were play-workers, activities such as swimming, going to the cinema and on outings, were organised. Where there were no play-workers, activities for children had to be organised by work with children was more sporadic. Lack of toys, bikes and go-carts was the main complaint of children interviewed of this age.

School holidays accentuated the lack of facilities. Nearly half the groups tried to organise special activities to take children out and local play-schemes were a godsend to those groups where there were no paid workers at all. Nearly a third of groups managed to organise a holiday for women and children. However, this was often difficult to arrange for financial reasons and also because any sort of long-term planning was impossible.

Teenagers in refuges

There were comparatively few teenage children in refuges at the time of the survey – there were none at all in a third of the refuges. Problems which did arise were either associated with schooling or the lack of facilities for them in the refuge and local area. Twenty seven per cent of groups reported problems with schooling of this age group*, particularly their acceptance into new schools, different syllabuses and the cost of providing new school uniforms. Many teenagers continued to go to their old school which meant travelling long distances at great expense with no financial aid. Where they did change schools, the disruption both socially and educationally was reported to more severe at this age. Many disliked being cut off from their own friends and social life, while lack of privacy made homework almost impossible. This problem became even more acute when exams were being taken.

The embarrassment of being in a refuge seemed to be greater at this age than any other. However some found it a great relief to be able to talk to other children with violent fathers and could admit fears and compare experiences without being embarrassed.

Children's general development in the refuge

Children of all ages coming to refuges had to cope with 2 things: leaving their home, usually their father, their school and friends, as well as arriving in a new and confusing situation. On arrival, many children showed the same relief as their mothers. Some had themselves been beaten by their fathers – 27% of women mentioned violence towards children as one of their reasons for leaving home. Children we interviewed were clearly happy to be away from the violence.

*Only 5% of groups said that fitting children under 11 into schools was difficult.

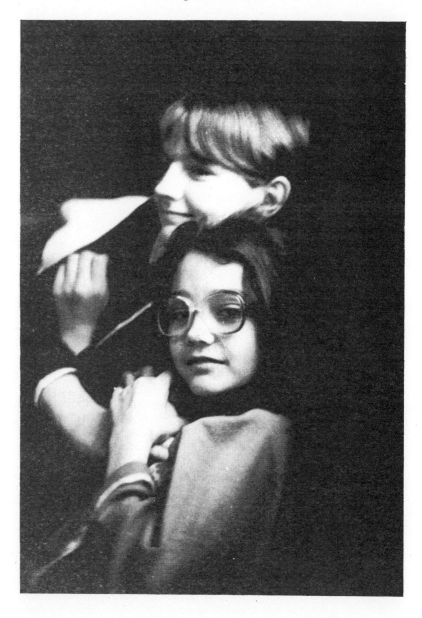

Close friends

'It's a lot easier in a refuge than being hit by your Dad. When I came in here I was very happy.'

Most children seemed to settle in fairly quickly. Babies tended to attract a lot of attention, while children of the 5–10 age group often seemed to regard their stay in the refuge as some sort of holiday. Typical comments were 'It's magic', 'It's really nice here', or 'I like having so many friends'. Some children were more critical however: 'It's too overcrowded, there's nowhere to be on your own and quiet and there's no toys for big boys.'

Many mothers described how their children had become less withdrawn and clinging since they came to the refuge, were 'less jumpy' and played more easily with other children. Toddlers were talking who had previously been regarded as slow developers and generally women thought their children were happier. Thirty five per cent of women thought their children had generally changed for the better, while 38% felt that they were much the same. Children's physical health had likewise improved more often than not, particularly in those areas of nervous illness made worse by stress, such as asthma. Habits such as bed-wetting and nail-biting had also decreased.

The other side of the story, however, is that children who are less withdrawn and nervous are much more noisy and boisterous. Most of the women who said their children had changed for the worse (27%) described them as having become 'cheeky', 'rude', or 'impossible'. One of the most difficult problems women had to cope with was the almost inevitable disruption of their usual patterns of discipline. Children were usually excited by their new surroundings and took advantage of their mother's state of mind to refuse normal bed-times and to 'play up'. They saw other children being allowed to do things they were forbidden to do and joined in. The poor state of repair in many refuges did not encourage respect from children, and mothers were often upset by destructive behaviour that their children 'wouldn't dream of doing at home'.

Summary

Lack of funding specifically for children meant that many refuges had no playspace or proper play equipment. Without paid play-workers, activities for children were limited and sporadic. Where Women's Aid groups had managed to obtain funding for children, the organised play provided for all age groups had greatly improved refuge life for both children and their mothers. Children played creatively in play-groups and play-rooms were stimulating places to spend time in rather than a mess of broken toys. Even where children's amenities were poor, however, children were still reported to be happier than they had been living with their fathers. Indeed, many children enjoyed their time in the refuge so much that they were miserable to leave their friends behind when they were rehoused.

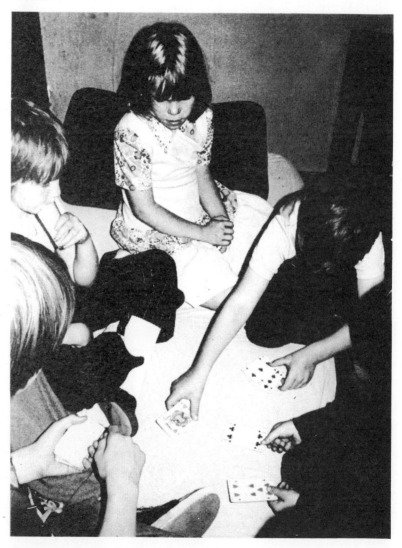

A quiet card game before bed-time.

8. Women's Attempts to Find Permanent Housing

We have seen that before coming to a refuge, women's attempts to leave home had often been thwarted by problems of accommodation. A third of women had approached housing departments in the past, with little or no success. The refuge gave women somewhere more secure from which to solve the problem of finding long-term accommodation, together with help and advice on their housing. However, refuges are intended as 'emergency' accommodation and were being hindered in their ability to function as such because of the length of time women had to wait in them.

Almost all the women using refuges (91%) wanted to leave their partner permanently and most (83%) had already taken steps to find permanent accommodation. Table 24 shows the ways in which they were trying to do so.

Table 24 : Ways women tried to find permanent housing

(as a percentage of the 514 women taking steps to secure housing)

418 women	81%	Local authorities
157	31%	Returning alone to former home
112 women	22%	Private renting
97 women	19%	Housing associations
32 women	6%	Other options

Note: 254 women (49%) were trying more than one route so there is some overlap.

The success or otherwise of women trying these different routes can be seen in Table 25 which shows where women went on leaving the refuge. Forty four per cent were rehoused by local authorities and a total of 63% found some form of permanent accommodation away from their violent partner. Fifteen per cent went on to other forms of emergency accommodation – hostels or with relatives and friends. Only 14% went back to their husband or boyfriend on leaving.

Table 25 : Destinations of women on leaving refuge†

Destination	%age on leaving refuge
Local Authority housing	44%
Previous home – man excluded	8%
Housing Association/private sector	11%
Still in refuge/hostel/Bed and Breakfast	9%
With relatives/friends	6%
Back to violent partner	14%
Unknown/other	8%
Total	100%

It can be seen that neither of the two most popular ways women were trying – obtaining local authority housing and excluding the partner from the previous home – were proving very successful. Yet it is in both these areas that recent legislation has sought to improve the position of battered women. The effects of the Housing (Homeless Persons) Act 1977 and the Domestic Violence Act 1976 are discussed below in the light of women's experiences and the opinions of groups running refuges.

The Housing (Homeless Persons) Act 1977

This Act imposed on housing authorities duties to offer some form of assistance to all homeless people, including women who have accommodation but cannot occupy it without risk of violence. Under the Act, an authority's obligation to secure accommodation for homeless persons extends only to those who are in priority need groups*, for example pregnant women and those with dependent children. That obligation is limited where the authority are satisfied the person became homeless intentionally†. Where a duty to secure accommodation does arise there is no specific requirement for the

†These figures are based on returns from 87 of the groups originally participating in the survey, and include 411 women.
*See section 2 of the Act.
†See section 17 of the Act.

Council to offer their accommodation. The Act additionally makes it clear that a woman may not be referred back to an authority in whose area she runs the risk of violence.

Altogether 81% of the women in our survey had applied to local authorities with 14% appliying to more than one authority. Not all women had approached the authority where their refuge was. Some had applied to the authority of the area they had lived in before coming to the refuge. In all, 75% of all local authority applications were to authorities where the woman was currently in a refuge, (called 'refuge local authorities') while a further 25% were to other housing authorities, including the GLC. This difference was to have a significant impact on the success of the application.

How were women's applications received

There were three elements to the reception of women's applications to local authorities. Firstly, there was the attitude of the housing officer to domestic violence and whether he/she saw it as a legitimate reason for women to leave home. Then there was the question of whether the woman was accepted for rehousing, in particular whether she was regarded as homeless or not and finally there was the process by which she was actually rehoused.

Attitudes of housing officials

As discussed in Chapter 2, one of the most common complaints of women approaching agencies for help was that they did not take the problem of battering seriously. Housing Departments were no exception and women often said they had been humiliated by the treatment they had received:

> 'They had no right to treat me as they did. I came out in tears many times, The housing officer says that he hits his wife and vice versa – and that's the way of a happy marriage.'

Were women treated as homeless

Altogether, 43% of applications were not accepted as being the responsibility of that Council under the Housing (Homeless Persons) Act. Almost a third of these were not even put on the ordinary waiting list. The reasons given for not agreeing to house women as homeless persons were:

Leaving Violent Men

Table 26 : Ways in which women were refused housing

Ways Applications Refused	No. of applications	%age of applic.
Told long wait on ordinary list ·	26	12%
Refused for ordinary list	34	15%
Defined as not homeless	71	32%
Responsibility of other authority	54	24%
Defined as not in priority need	21	9%
Said to be intentionally homeless	18	8%
Total	207†	100%

It is impossible to know from this survey the exact extent to which this high refusal rate was due to authorities legitimately using their discretion under the Act or to their being negligent in meeting their legal obligations. Some councils made no mention of the Act to the women concerned. A closer look at those cases where the Act was referred to in turning women away, sheds some further light on the issue.

a. Women defined as not homeless

Deciding that women were 'not homeless' was the most common reason given for refusal. Some women were told that they were not battered because they could not show visible bruising or produce evidence of assault. Some were given no reasons at all. In other cases it was argued that, although women were battered, they were not homeless since they had accommodation in the refuge:

> 'They said there was a 2–5 year waiting list for housing, that we weren't really in need. They said there were people living on the street who need a house – at least we had a roof over our heads . . .'

A refuge is, by its nature, emergency accommodation and for the purposes of the Act it should not be acceptable to argue that being in a refuge means a woman is no longer homeless. However some authorities still appeared to be using that argument.

b. Women defined as the responsibility of another area

The women's reports suggested that many authorities were still refusing to rehouse battered women from outside their area.* These women were being sent back to areas where they were in danger of

---

†Seventeen women had been given more than one of the above reasons by the same authority, so the number of applications refused is 207.
*And were failing to follow the notification procedure laid down in Section 8 of the Act. Women were simply left to contact the new authority themselves.

further violence. There were several cases of women being shunted back and forth between two authorities with neither being prepared to give in and accept responsibility for them. Remarks such as 'we've had two families from your area and we don't want any more' were not uncommon, showing local authority fears of being taken advantage of by less responsible authorities.

c. Women defined as not in priority need

Pregnant woman were sometimes being turned away as 'not in priority need'. However this argument was mostly used against women without dependent children. Such women were seldom rehoused, despite the fact that they could be considered as 'vulnerable' under the Act, due to their history of being battered and the fact that they were in danger of further attacks. The failure of some authorities to offer even adequate advice to this group* is illustrated by the woman who said:

> 'They told me to go to London where there are plenty of hostels.'

d. Women said to be intentionally homeless

Finally, some women were refused housing on the grounds that they had become homeless intentionally, although there seemed to be little justification for this. One woman was told that she had 'left the marital home of her own free will', while another said:

> 'My husband told them he'd offered me the house three times and they believed him.'

Some councils called women intentionally homeless if they turned down the first offer of accommodation, no matter how bad it was. One woman said 'the group turned it down on sight because the property was derelict'. And another:

> 'I was so angry, the third offer was so terrible but he (Homelessness Officer) said "If you were homeless you'd take it".'

Many of these findings suggest that to some extent battered women's housing needs are not always taken seriously, and that there is a belief that in the end they will go back home. In fact the survey showed that only 14% of women went back to husbands on leaving refuges, and only 6% of those given permanent accommodation had gone back to husbands eighteen months later.

---

*Contrary to Section 4-2/a of the Act. The Code of Guidance accompanying the Act recommends that battered women without children be considered to be in priority need wherever possible.

Leaving Violent Men

The process of rehousing

Another problem area concerned women who had been told to fulfil certain criteria before they could be rehoused.† Twenty per cent of women mentioned having to obtain a divorce or custody of children before the authority would accept them. Councils were also demanding that women have the tenancy of their previous home transferred to their name or pay off rent arrears (14% of applications) before they would be considered for rehousing. Such criteria* frequently caused long delays and some women were excluded from housing because they could not meet the conditions laid down. One woman who had had to wait in the refuge for over a year told us:

> 'In the end I had only two minutes for custody in the office and still had to wait six weeks for the divorce. I was so mad! After all the months I'd waited and all the fuss of the court welfare. I got custody of the two-year-old and him of the nine-year-old – eventually I was offered this place and the worker said, "If you don't take it you'll get slum clearance".'

Some women chose to have the previous tenancy transferred to them, since they could then swap it for better quality accommodation than they would be offered as homeless persons. Others however, were being forced to pursue this roundabout route to rehousing which often led to rent arrears.

Rent arrears† were frequently built up in the process of women leaving home. Men defaulted on the rent after their wives or girlfriends left them, and women often had little say in whether or not the rent was paid before they left home, since they did not control the money. Women were then held responsible for all or part of these arrears, particularly if the tenancy was transferred to their name. While in the refuge waiting to be offered another tenancy, women were responsible for two rents, and the longer it took to rehouse them, the more arrears built up:

> 'I went to them in August and it wasn't until the back of Christmas I found I didn't stand a chance until I'd paid off the arrears from the other place. I had to pay off the arrears through a charity before they would consider me as a priority. Although three quarters of the arrears weren't accumulated by me, it was my husband. That was one of the reasons I left him.'

†In surveys of local authority housing policies carried out by Welsh Women's Aid, and Scottish Women's Aid, similar criteria were found to operate before battered women could be rehoused.
*Custody was said to be a major problem by 25% of groups, tenancy transfers by 52% and rent arrears by 25%.
†Rent arrears had built up on the former homes of 37% of women in the survey.

Many groups felt strongly that the problem of rent arrears demanded a broader solution than simply holding individual battered women responsible. Women had had little control over whether they were built up and the arrears severely interfered with their chances of rehousing. Women were sometimes left with debts of £200 or £300 to be paid off out of social security payments, already considered to be the minimum subsistence level. This, together with the fact that they had often lost all their belongings, made leaving home an expensive business for many battered women. The DHSS is empowered to pay two rents simultaneously to a claimant, under special circumstances, but few Women's Aid groups had been able to secure this concession for women living in their refuges.

Women had made better progress and were more satisfied when they had approached the council where the refuge was, regardless of whether they originally came from that area or not. It may be that having a Women's Aid group on the spot to back up the application was more important than a previous connection with the area. Some groups had developed a good relationship with the local housing department over the years and reached agreements to ensure the smooth rehousing of women from their refuge. Others, who felt the authority was not giving battered women a fair deal, acted as 'watchdogs' and put pressure on it to accept them as an obligation under the Housing (Homeless Persons) Act. As one group told us:

'S. Council always comes up with the same story, "there is no housing available" and "we are doing the best we can with the limited supply". We fight continually about their interpretation of the Housing Act.'

In some cases it was another agency who put pressure on the Housing Department:

'I was going down to the office regularly asking them but nothing happened. Eventually I went to the Law Centre and they wrote to the Council threatening to take them to court for breaking the Homeless Persons Act. They gave me an offer two days later.'

In all, only a quarter of women were satisfied with the treatment they had received from local authorities. Women were taking on average 6 months to find permanent accommodation and the follow-up study shows that even those who were being rehoused as homeless persons stayed on average 5 months in refuges. 15% of women in the survey stayed in refuges longer than a year because of lack of anywhere to go.

The prospects of battered women getting rehoused before and after the Housing (Homeless Persons) Act

It has been argued that battered women are among those who have definitely benefitted from the Act[19] but the evidence from this and other surveys questions the extent to which this is true.

Less than half the Women's Aid groups thought that the housing prospects of women in their refuge had improved since the Act came into effect. Some groups said that it had actually become more difficult for women since the Act, because authorities had tightened up their criteria in an attempt to limit their responsibilities. Eighteen months later, many groups felt that the gains from the Housing (Homeless Persons) Act were only temporary and have since been eroded as a result of local authority spending cuts. For example, during the follow-up study, we found that the length of time women had to wait in refuges for local authority accommodation had increased in many areas of the country from six months to a year – particularly in London. A Women's Aid group in the West Country stated in June 1980:

> 'Two years ago we were getting local women rehoused after three months waiting period, and those outside the area after six months. Now we can't get anyone from outside the area rehoused, and even women from here have over a year to wait.'

A special examination of the local authorities' homelessness returns to the Department of the Environment for 1978* showed that battered women, once accepted as homeless were receiving different treatment from other homeless groups. Fewer battered women were rehoused directly and excluding those referred to a hostel or refuge, more were put into Bed and Breakfast accommodation. This may well reflect the emergency nature of marital violence and the need to act quickly, but it could also suggest that the housing departments are testing women to see whether they are seriously intending to stay separated.

Other reviewers support the view that battered women are getting a worse deal than other homeless groups:

> 'Some authorities are taking a comparatively hard line toward these people . . . making every effort to try and induce them to return to their former homes and advocating the use of the rather limited remedies contained in the 1976 Domestic Violence Act.'[11]

---

*Source: DOE Homelessness Statistics, unpub.

'Although the Act is by and large being implemented, the provision of facilities for battered wives and persons at sexual or financial risk are to some extent inadequate and there is considerable scope for improvement in attitude and facilities for this very specific area of the Act.'[12]

The Domestic Violence Act – returning to the previous home

After seeking rehousing from the local authority the next most popular solution sought by women in our survey was trying to obtain the previous home with the violent partner excluded. The Domestic Violence Act was intended to make a woman's home safe for her to live in, by excluding the violent partner with a court injunction.† It has been claimed that this Act presents the most appropriate way for battered women to secure long-term housing.[14] However the Act offers only a temporary solution and our study has high-lighted two drawbacks in practice. Firstly, it was not so easy to get an exclusion order; the violence has to be proved severe before the judges will consider throwing a man out of the joint home, and even more severe and persistent for police powers of arrest to be attached to the injunction. Eighty-two women were applying for exclusion orders. Forty five per cent had been granted them, while others were still waiting to be heard.* Five women had been refused exclusion orders altogether, while others had not been granted powers of arrest:

> 'I went to court but they said my husband must have a room in the house as it's in both names.'

> 'I've had difficulty getting it (exclusion order), because he denies charges.'

Several other women had been denied legal aid to even apply for an exclusion order, one despite a 25 year history of domestic violence.

The second drawback to the Domestic Violence Act is the difficulty of having injunctions enforced. Many women and Women's Aid groups felt that without police powers of arrest, injunctions were worthless, since there was little to deter a man from breaking one. Women reported that the police had been reluctant to answer calls for help in the event of a broken injunction, and even more reluctant to press charges. (See Chapter 2 of this report). The sentences men received when charged, were felt to be so trivial that women had not

†We are concerned here with exclusion orders rather than non-molestation orders, because of their relevance to women's accommodation needs.
*NWAF found in April 1978 that of 58 women who had applied for exclusion orders, only 21 were granted them.[22]

bothered to use an injunction again. In September 1978. 32 women who had obtained exclusion orders were still living in refuges, either because they were too afraid to move back home or because the men refused to move out:

'I got the injunction. My husband says he'll be back after a few days, so I'm scared to go back.'

'I have an injunction with powers of arrest, but I can't get him out.'

'They won't attach powers of arrest until I'm living there permanently and he tries to get in. I've been back twice and he's broken in both times.'

Although a third of women in the survey were trying to get rights over their previous homes,* either to live in or to transfer for another tenancy, only 16% of all the women wanted to live in their previous home again. Most felt that they would be unsafe there or that bad memories of the place and the response of neighbours would make it difficult to start life afresh. In many cases, women were under pressure from local authorities to use this route to housing – the number of authorities reported to be using the existence of the Domestic Violence Act as grounds for refusing to rehouse battered women had risen from six to 13 (out of 114) since the Housing (Homeless Persons) Act came into effect. However, in our survey this route to permanent housing was not proving a viable option for most women – out of 411 women, only 8% finally left refuges to return to their previous homes without their partners and one year after the interviews, only half that number were still there.

Summary

To summarise, then, the two main housing options open to battered women were not successfully catering for the needs of women in refuges. Returning to the previous home with the partner excluded is not at present a viable alternative for most women and requires much stricter enforcement of injunctions if women are to make use of it. The majority of women did not want to return to their former homes in any case. This left most women with the option of approaching local authorities as homeless persons, but the Housing (Homeless Persons) Act was failing to cater for a substantial proportion of them. In our survey, at least 43% of applications to councils had been refused, and even where they had been accepted, long delays and further obstacles confronted women before they were

*Not all women were using the DVA to do this, others had gone direct to the council.

rehoused. Only 44% of women left the refuge to move into Council property although twice that number had applied. It is hardly surprising that only a quarter of women were satisfied with the treatment they had received from local authorities. The Act has had some limited gains for battered women in refuges, but there is considerable room for improvement. It cannot be claimed that these gains are general to all battered women, since the lobbying of councils by Women's Aid groups seemed to play an important part in eventually securing housing for women in refuges. The Act has not had as dramatic an effect on battered women's housing prospects as might have been expected and there is evidence that they are receiving worse treatment than other homeless groups.

9. Women's Housing After Leaving the Refuge

A year after being interviewed, two thirds of the women were in the same place that they had moved to on leaving the refuge. The most stable group were those who found permanent separate accommodation, different from their previous homes (78% still in same place). The least stable groups were those who went on to other forms of emergency accommodation (35%) and those who went back to their previous homes with their partner excluded (50% still in same place). Disturbingly, 6% of women in the follow-up study were still in emergency forms of accommodation 18 months after first being interviewed.

Table 28 : Women's destinations on leaving refuge and 1 year after interview.

Destination	% on leaving refuge	% 1 year after interview
In a new home - either temporary or permanent accommodation	55%	49%
In previous home – partner excluded	8%	4%
Still in emergency accommodation – hostel, refuge, bed and breakfast	15%	9%
Back with violent partner	14%	16%
Unknown	8%	22%
Total:	100%	100%

Figures on 411 women traced a year later.

In this chapter we look at those women who had found new homes – their tenure, the quality of the housing, and its suitability for their needs. Although only 44% of women moved into Council housing, this was still the major source of permanent accommodation for women leaving refuges.

Table 29 : Tenure of women in new homes

Tenure	no.	%
Council	47	83
Housing Association	7	12
Private Rented	3	5
Total	57	100%

The type of housing women obtained

The properties ranged a great deal in age, type and basic condition. Twenty per cent were pre-war, 34% inter-war and 41% post-war. As regards type of property, 29% were terraced houses, 25% semi-detached and 33% flats. 9% were maisonettes. Only 54% of properties had a garden or yard of their own, despite the fact that most women had young children.

Nineteen per cent of women in the survey had in fact turned down at least one offer of accommodation because it was so poor. But most women felt obliged to accept the first offer they were made, since they were usually told that if they turned it down, they would be classed as 'intentionally homeless'.

43% of women described their present accommodation as poor. In many cases the properties had been derelict or vandalised:

'There was no paper on the walls anywhere – holes in the walls, the floor stunk of piss. It was like walking into a men's toilet. One of the sockets was open, all the wires showing. I had to get a friend to do that. And there was a dirty crack down the middle of the ceiling in one bedroom.'

In all, 70% of the properties were said to have needed repairs doing to them when women moved in. It had taken on average five months to get Councils to do the work, although some women had waited as long as 18 months and others were still waiting:

'It wasn't bad, but there was damp in the bedroom and the back-boiler didn't heat water. I asked the council to fix the boiler and the damp and they only did it the day before I left, after waiting a year.'

In some cases women had been left for long periods without the most basic amenities such as heating, bath or toilet, in working order.

Other features of properties that women disliked, were poor or inadequate heating (28%) and cramped conditions (20%). Damp

houses were difficult to heat and women could usually only afford to
heat one room. Those dependent entirely on electric heaters could
hardly afford to use them.

Many women said there was nothing they liked about the property
except that it was a 'roof over our heads'. One of the women who
now regretted having accepted the property in the first place, said:

'I like it because it's mine – that's the only thing about it. That's all!'

Those women who were happy with their new homes (40%)
usually mentioned the space, ease of cleaning and the fact that it was
newly built or recently modernised. In other cases, houses with faults
were made more acceptable by other good features, such as gardens:

'It's just small enough to manage but big enough for me and my kiddies. I
like the position and all. I've got grass all around and roses in the front
and blackberries and raspberries in the back, so why should I argue.'

Just over half the women described their present housing as worse
than where they had lived before going to a refuge, while 39% said it
was better. For instance, one woman left a spacious modern home,
with a garden. She was now high up in a block of flats with no lift and
had had to do all the repairs herself. Many of the women who
preferred their present house described living in very run-down, poor
quality housing beforehand.

Sixty eight per cent said that, given the chance, they would move.
This was generally because of the poor state of the property or the
area. Others, although they had complaints, said they would not
move because of the amount of work they had put into making the
place habitable or because they could not face unsettling their lives
again.

In any case, the prospect of getting transferred to a better property
was usually bleak, especially for those in the poorest housing.

Decoration and basic amenities

Most women were on very low incomes and were starting á new
home with very few possessions.† However, houses in poor structural
condition, with crumbling plaster or damp walls, were exceedingly
difficult to make habitable by decorating and they required far more
skill and financial outlay than those simply requiring a coat of paint.
Even where properties were in good condition, the cost of decoration
could be prohibitive for a family on social security, unless grants were

† See chapter 10.

forthcoming. In some cases, councils had given money towards the cost of decoration or had allowed a.few weeks rent free to compensate, but these amounts, £30-£60, seldom came near the actual cost involved. One woman said she had been let off the rent for two weeks by the council, only to find that, as a consequence, the DHSS withdrew her rent allowance for that period.

Furnishings were often minimal – interviewers often used words such as 'sparse', 'spartan', or 'bare', to describe the homes they visited. Long after moving in, many women could still not afford floor coverings, cupboards or chests of drawers.

The areas where women were rehoused

The areas where women had been rehoused varied considerably, from rural, cottage estates to run-down 'problem-family' areas or half boarded up, re-development zones, as this selection of interviewers' descriptions shows:

> 'It was a new estate of about 10 blocks of terraced houses in Stainforth – very quiet and respectable. Little grass lawns extending along the front of the terrace and small back yards.'

> 'A very depressing block of flats, glass broken on landings, windows and main doors, rubbish on the stairs. Awful, worst place I've seen.'

> 'The house was in a rickety, old cobbled street near the city centre, due for redevelopment. It was the only house in a row of little shops and light industries. A huge complex of modern blocks of flats loomed over it from across the road.'

The immediate neighbourhood strongly influenced how happy women felt with the housing they had been given. Convenience for shops, buses and social amenities was important to women, most of whom had small children and relied mostly on public transport. Areas that were 'too posh' or 'too rough' made it difficult for women to make social contacts or to feel at ease in their new surroundings.

In common with other findings[18] the women complained that there was nowhere for children to play, particularly those living in flats. In 'rough' areas, women living on their own were tormented by gangs of children, usually teenage boys. Bricks and rubbish were thrown at the house, women were taunted in the street and their children terrorised:

> 'Every time I go out something happens. The kids put the windows in. Last year, when I'd just moved in, they tried to set fire to my outshed. They started a fire on my front doorstep, they're always beating my son up.'

Women were very aware of the fact that this sort of behaviour went further than usual because children knew there wasn't a man in the house to go and 'put an end to all the nonsense'. One woman had taken her husband back because she felt the area was unsafe for a woman living alone.

Battered women have often left their previous homes suddenly or secretly, bringing little with them. They may have moved to a town where they knew no-one outside the refuge. They therefore valued the proximity of essential services and social contacts. Not surprisingly they wanted to live near friends and relatives or close to women they had met in the refuge. They did not however want to be close to their partners, but were often given no choice in the matter, in spite of the fact that many were still in danger of further violent attacks.

> 'They offered me a flat opposite where my husband was working but I had to take it in the end because I wouldn't have been given another flat. I had to take this flat opposite where he worked – they knew about this but wouldn't change it. I knew my life was in danger.'

Summary

Some women were satisfied with the housing they had obtained, but many others had accepted properties out of desperation and more than two thirds wanted to move. Structural faults were common and little help had been forthcoming from councils for repairs, decoration or cleaning the property, even when it had been vandalised or left empty for a long time.

Proximity to friends, relatives or the refuge as well as to essential services could greatly effect how well a woman had settled into her new home. Many battered women who leave home are in danger of further violent attacks. This makes it preferable for them to be rehoused away from their husband's neighbourhood and sometimes from the area altogether.

10. Starting Again in a New Home

There was a sharp contrast between living in the refuge and being rehoused alone with one's children*. Sharing with so many other women and children, always having someone to talk to and feeling safe from a violent attack, were suddenly lost. It was not an experience most women had enjoyed:

'The privacy and the quiet was quite nice but the loneliness to start off with was pretty bad – I found I went back to the refuge quite a lot in the first fortnight – every day in fact.'

By the time of the follow-up study†, life had usually settled into a routine and it was possible to see how women felt about their new lives and the social contacts they had made. Of those living alone, the majority (65%) said they enjoyed doing so. They valued the freedom to do what they wanted:

'I'm quite happy being a one-parent family. My social life's my own. I'm much stronger now and I'm happy with my life as it is at the moment. I'm free completely – as far as you can be with two children. I get low at times but now I'm not married and I'm on my own I know it will be much better for me.'

'You're your own boss. Nobody to pick you up on your faults and give you a black eye for it. You can shop for what you need and the kids can go on school trips and to youth clubs.'

*Seventy women had been rehoused and most had experienced living alone, at least to start with. Eighteen women were now living with different men, 7 were living with relatives, friends, or were in a refuge or hostel, and 45 were living on their own when interviewed.
†Interviews took place 18 months after the previous interview in the refuge. Most women had been rehoused for at least a year by this time.

Although women did like living alone, there were times when they felt very lonely. Unless they had someone to share childcare with, they were often forced to stay in the home the whole day:

> 'I get a bit low stuck here all day, with the kids, cos I don't go out much – I keep thinking there must be more to life than this. I'm sat here like a bloomin' old granny knitting away but apart from that, I've got the girls and we talk alot. It's not bad really.'

Only four women positively disliked living alone:

> 'I feel sorry for the kids just having me – I can't give them as much as they want. The kids feel very insecure – it's not a family just with me.'

Having a paid job had helped some women to overcome their loneliness. However, of those women living alone, half still felt lonely even when they had a job.

Contact with neighbours could make all the difference. About a third of women seemed to be on close terms with neighbours, i.e. they talked to them at least once a day, sometimes went shopping with them or collected each other's children from school. But on some estates women said they often spoke to no-one at all, making help with harassing husbands difficult:

> 'He tried to strangle me once at the front door. I bit his hand and screamed and the neighbour came out. She says: "What did you scream for?" I says: "Because I wanted help". And she says: "Well you can't scream like that cos my husband's got a bad heart", and just went in.'

Isolation was often made worse where women were rehoused miles from the refuge or from anyone close they knew, especially if they came from another town in the first place. Such difficulties have important implications for rehousing policy. Women's Aid groups, have been encouraging housing departments to rehouse women close to each other. Where this had happened, strong support networks have developed. In many ways this proved more helpful to women once they left the refuge, than keeping contact with the refuge itself.

For those women not rehoused close to each other, Women's Aid was still an important source of social contacts. A third of women still went to the refuge, sometimes for a weekly coffee morning for ex-residents, or were now involved in the support group.

Encouraging social contact amongst women who had left was felt to be important by Women's Aid groups but most did not have the resources to organise this. One group had managed to get Manpower Service Commission funding to start a centre for ex-residents. Problems with housing, health, employment and child-care were taiked over together and the friendly atmosphere encouraged women to pop in and out whenever they wanted.

Providing such a meeting plåce or rehousing women close together offered women company and a chance to talk over any worries. Women's Aid contacts were more often mentioned as a source of help than other contacts such as friends and relatives (Table 24), and half the women interviewed would have liked more contact with Women's Aid.

Table 30 : Contacts found most helpful to women since leaving the refuge

	No. of Women	%age
Someone they knew from the refuge	22	31%
Relative	11	16%
Friend	10	14%
New partner	10	14%
Other	6	9%
No-one	11	16%
Total	70	100%

Given the difficulties of socialising outside the home, would women have preferred to have someone else living with them? The idea of joint tenancies with other families was quite popular. Over a third would have liked to share their home with another family. Over half were opposed to the idea, while the remainder were unsure. It is particularly interesting that the idea was most popular amongst women who had returned to their husbands – 60% of these said they would have taken a tenancy with a friend if they had been offered one in the refuge. This suggests that women had returned home more out of loneliness and the difficulties of coping on their own than for their feelings for their partner.

Children in their new homes

Eighty four per cent of women had sole custody of their children, the number of children they had ranging from one to eight, averaging two–three each.

Incomes for most women in this survey were well below average and for those on social security, it was impossible to provide the things they would have liked for their children. Day trips were often out of the question and only a quarter of women had gone on holiday the previous summer, often organised by the refuge. Ninety per cent of the remainder could not afford it and many had not had a holiday for years – if ever.

Money

Moving into a new home is an expensive business for anyone. Women from refuges however, were starting from scratch. They had often had little opportunity to pack up their things when they left home. All the basic furniture had to be bought – cookers, beds, tables and chairs, carpets and curtains. Most women had been dependent on social security since they had left home.

In all, 67 women applied to DHSS for an exceptional needs payment out of 70 who had moved into a new home:

Table 31 : Grants applied for and obtained from the DHSS

	No. of women who applied	%age	No. of women who obtained	%age
Clothing grant	49	74%	37	59%
Furniture grant	55	83%	47	75%
Removal expenses	9	19%	7	16%

(women could apply for all 3 grants above)

Total: 70 women

As exceptional needs payments were discretionary,* there was a big variation in what women received both within one refuge and regionally.† Total grants in all these categories ranged from £14 to £450 and averaged £142. Three women were refused all grants available.

Many women, although relieved to gain some help from DHSS, were dissatisfied with the way they had been treated:

'Social Security said to me: "What have you got?" and I said: "Nothing" and she said : "Oh". And then I said: "Actually my husband did burn all the things in the garden". "Oh", she says, "he can't do that", but I says: "He's already done it!" So she says: "You should have gone and fetched your things when you left". She couldn't understand why I didn't stand there and say: "I want that, that and that". I said: "He'd have *killed* me". I don't think they believe you.'

Setting up a new home was the first financial hurdle women had to overcome. How were they managing 18 months later? As seen below,

*Under the Social Security Act 1980 exceptional needs payments have been replaced by a single payment for laid down categories of need. It is not clear how this will effect the position of battered women.

†Four women got over £350 in one refuge in East Anglia, while the average grant received by women in a refuge in the Manchester area was £50. In one Midlands town, no women had received furniture grants at all.

the majority of women who had separated permanently were still living as single parents on social security while 18 were living with a new partner:

Table 32 : Source of income and amount approximately 18 months after being housed

Source of income	No. of women	% of women	Usual weekly income (take home)
Social Security	41	56%	£45**
Job	10	14%	£59
Combined income with new partner – job or Social Security	18	25%	£79
Widow's Pension*	3	4%	£58
Maintenance	1	1%	not given
	73	100%	£60 – on average

*Three husbands had died and these women were amongst the most well-off in the survey.
**This amount includes money for rent and children's allowances. The average rent paid by women on social security was £13 and they had an average of 2 children.

Battered women shared with other one-parent families difficulties which have been documented by the Finer Committee.[14] Finding money for the basic necessities like food, bills and clothes was the biggest problem. Bills all seemed to come in at the same time and many women had moved from quarterly bills for gas and electricity to meters to avoid getting into debt. Children grew out of clothes quickly and even a trip to a jumble sale could take too much out of a weekly budget.

Although women had often obtained some grant for furnishings when they had moved in, many just hadn't been able to "get on their feet financially" and still lived in bare rooms with no carpets or curtains:

'The school playleader came round and says: "Oh you've not got a carpet" – I says: "I know I haven't". She says: "Why not" and I says: "I can't slap a bit of Axminster between 2 slices of bread and say to my kids there's your tea!"'

Ten women living alone with their child or children had a job. Most women wanted to work but lack of child-care and lack of jobs prevented many of them from doing so.* Although the pay for those

*See the Welsh Women's Aid Survey 1980[24] for a detailed discussion of the employment prospects of women who have been through refuges.

who had a job was on average slightly higher than those on social security, there were disadvantages. Women working were not eligible for emergency needs payments and had had to furnish their new homes with no help from DHSS.

Most women did unskilled manual work and were thus amongst the lowest paid workers in the country. Supplying everything for a family on one income was proving difficult for these women too, and again led to the occassional non-payment of rent on special occasions, like Christmas and birthdays.

Eighteen women were now living with a new partner. The combined family income was over £30 a week more on average than that for women alone on social security. This led to some improvements in lifestyle particularly for extras like holidays or going out socially. However, five families were dependent on social security or unemployment benefit so were experiencing the same level of poverty as the women living alone.

Thus most women were very hard up even 18 months later, whether they were on social security, had a job or a new partner. Yet in spite of their low incomes, two thirds of the women said they were better off now than when they were living with their previous partner. As we saw in Chapter 1 some women had been kept in absolute poverty before they left home. Any regular stable income was therefore an improvement.

Safety after women had separated

Escaping from violence is not automatically achieved by separating from a violent partner. While some men (59%) left their partners alone, others continued to harass them while they were in the refuge and when they were rehoused. Some women were still being harassed 18 months later and had been forced to leave their new home and live in a refuge or homeless families hostel. Not suprisingly, as can be seen in Table 33 women were more likely to be harassed where their address was known by their old partners.

Keeping women's new address secret from their ex-husband

Obtaining separate accommodation from the Council or a Housing Association had been a long and frustrating experience for many women. It took one small slip-up in court or a chance give-away by a friend for the new address to be revealed to the ex-husband. Violence often began again and the woman was back where she started. Two-thirds of men now knew their ex-wives new address.

One woman who had been rehoused twice and moved from refuge

to refuge to escape her husband, was finally allocated another house 200 miles from her previous home. Children were settled in school and liked the town. Despite her long history of trying to escape, a social worker told her husband where she was and she was forced to flee yet again with her six children, this time to Scotland.

Men most frequently learnt of their wives' whereabouts through contact with children. Addresses would be given at court hearings over custody, or men would follow children home after access. Sometimes young children were asked to show Dad their new home and they proudly did so. Usually, however, the indiscretions came from agencies working regularly with battered women and shows again their tendency not to take domestic violence seriously enough.

Even women who had managed to keep their new address secret did not always feel safe:

> 'If he knew where I was now, he'd be here tomorrow and the children would be gone. I was in hospital having an emergency operation because of what he'd done to me – he found the children and I didn't see them for the next four months. That's the type of person he is.'

The effect on women's safety if the husband found her new address can be seen below:

Table 33: Effect on women's safety of secrecy being lost

	Women harassed No.	%	Women not harassed No.	%
Address known by ex-partner	26	53%	23	47%
Address not known	3	14%	18	86%
Totals	29	41%	41	59%

Once traced, many women could expect a good deal of harassment from their old partners. Men usually used a mixture of conciliatory gestures and threats, violence often being used when women refused to take them back. More than half of those traced had suffered some sort of trouble since they had been separated, while 15 had been attacked:

> 'My address was read out in court. I couldn't believe it. The solicitor *told* them not to. He used to come up here harassing me. He wired my washing machine up when I was out to blow up and then he had second thoughts about it and told the police to tell me not to go home. He's tried to strangle me. It was as bad as before I left him but I was more frightened here because I didn't know anyone.'

Harassment had arisen particularly in connection with access to children. This seemed to be a way in which many men could continue to threaten and bully their ex-wives. Arrangements to pick up children were broken, women kept waiting at stations and bus stops for children to be returned and arguments and sometimes violence would ensue.

Nearly half the men had had some arrangement to see their children at least when they first separated. Eighteen months later though, many fathers had ceased to have any relationship with them. If the children had a good relationship with their father, women felt guilty if they refused them access. However a third still felt threatened by this contact with him:

'I can't see what right I have to deprive them of their dad but if he's seeing them there's always a chance he'll be violent to me.'

Protection afforded women by the police and courts

What protection, then, is currently available to battered women against their ex-husbands once they have separated? As we saw in Chapter 2, the police were reluctant to charge men for violence against their wives in the matrimonial home. Now they were separated one would expect that the assault would no longer be dismissed as a "domestic dispute". Sixty six per cent of women interviewed 18 months later were now either divorced from their previous husband or in the process of obtaining a divorce and 17% had never been married anyway.

All but one of the women physically attacked since leaving the refuge, had called the police; others had done so after harassment or threats of violence. However, there seemed to be little change in police response to calls for help – a placatory role was usually adopted:

'He punched me about, I had a knife at my throat, just things like that, just generally what he usually does. I called the police but they never arrested him. I asked them to take him back to Derby but they didn't. They offered him a cup of tea – I live here but they offered him a cup of tea – and then they put him out in the garden and he was there all night throwing stones and shouting. And my face was out here (with bruising).
(woman rehoused with non-molestation order and exclusion order both with powers of arrest).

Eight of the 15 women attacked already had injunctions but this did not seem to improve their chances of protection much:

'At first I only got a non-molestation order without powers of arrest. Then he tried to get into my flat – threatened me with a knife and said he'd kill me this time. The police said they couldn't help unless I had a powers of arrest clause.'

With injunctions usually failing to offer protection, women resorted to other methods of coping with harassment, often relying, not always successfully, on neighbours.

Summary

Starting a new life had not been easy for most women. Although the difficulties were greatest when they first moved out of the refuge, loneliness, harassment and poverty continued to beset them long after this. Despite these problems, almost all the women still separated were pleased that they had made the break and felt that their refuge experience had given them new confidence. Overwhelmingly women felt that both they (93%) and their children (83%) were much happier than they had been before leaving their husband.

Much could still be done to improve the situation of women who leave violent partners. Sensitive rehousing policies could ensure that social contacts from the refuge were maintained, while better police protection could cut down fear and harassment. However, only a more adequate system of social assistance for one-parent families, together with better access to jobs and child-care facilities, could improve the gruelling poverty in which most of these women were forced to live.

11. Returning to Husbands or Boyfriends

Only nine women (11%) in the follow-up study were back with their previous partners, but it was felt to be important to record their experience in some detail, since so few studies of violence in the home have included women still living with violent partners. A further five had lived with the men at some point between the first and second interviews, but were now living alone. Six out of the nine women now with their partner wanted to leave him again and one woman was doing so the day after the interview. This confirms the Dobash's view[1] that leaving a violent relationship is a process which can take some time and which may involve leaving and returning several times. Given the pressures experienced by women living on their own, (see Chapter 10) the number of women back with their husband or boyfriend was surprisingly low.

Why had these women gone back to violent partners? The reasons were similar to those women gave for returning home in the past (see Chapter 1), although lack of accommodation was a less common reason this time. In some cases, a man had promised to reform and women wanted to give him another chance. He still had a 'nice side', or she simply felt sorry for him or responsible for his well-being:

'When I met him 10 years ago, he had so many problems and I ironed out so many of these I felt I couldn't see it all go down the drain.'

'I felt after a year I still loved him. I was hoping he'd changed 'cos after a year I'd really grown up and thought if he hadn't changed, I could leave again, knowing that I could do it. I proved I could. I'm glad I left him and glad I came back.'

In other cases women acknowledged that they had gone back solely because of the pressures of trying to make a life on their own – either over-crowding in the refuge, the struggle to make ends meet or sheer loneliness:

'I was very lonely before he came back. It was terrible, especially in the winter. I think an adult needs an adult for company. You read books which tell you to go out, but they're written by people who haven't got a clue, because you can't go out because you haven't got any money.'

One woman did not have her children with her in the refuge and missed them too much to wait until she got a house. Another said:

'I went back because my life was so appalling in the refuge.'

Two women had simply been forced back with their partners, out of fear or his persistence. They felt they were no freer from him when they were living apart. One man simply wouldn't give up: he broke the door of her new flat down, burned the flat out and took an overdose on her premises. The woman now seemed to accept him as some kind of fate. Although she wanted to live on her own because he was so domineering and violent, she had no immediate plans to do anything about it.

Did women feel their men's behaviour had improved now they were back together? Most women said that things were better for the first few weeks, but that this 'honeymoon period' had seldom lasted long. Four women felt that in the long run, the relationship was worse now than before they had left.

Eight of the 13 women who had been back felt that the relationship had improved in some way after their refuge stay, but only one woman was happy with the extent of the improvement:

'He's changed. He's not the same man. He sees me as an equal, not as a dependent. He knows I can, and would, go if he tried to treat me the same way again. He's really grown up and learned a lot.'

Nine of the 13 women said their partner had been violent towards them since they got back together, usually on several occasions:

'He was great at first, when he was coming here for odd days – except for his drinking. He has a drink problem. Then he moved back – there's only been the one time he's hit me, with the hammer, but he doesn't seem to be able to take the responsibility of having to consider me and the kids.'

Some women seemed to cope with being back by keeping out of their husband's way. A few women said they particularly did not like going out with their partner socially, because of his behaviour in public – getting drunk, insulting her or ignoring her. Only one woman said that she would talk to her husband if she was upset about something and six said there was no-one they felt they could talk to. Several wished they had kept contact with the refuge:

'I wish I'd had more contact. I think, if I'd seen Mary (refuge worker) or somebody more, I wouldn't have been in the state I was when she came to my house. I was in a terrible state – I was a real nervous wreck.'

The social life of most of these women was very restricted, apart from the few who had paid jobs. Seven of the 11 we asked, never went out socially in the evenings and only one woman went out more than once a month. Daytime contact with neighbours or friends was infrequent and nine women described themselves as lonely, five desperately so:

'I'm cut off, just like all the other times. He expects me to be with him, not to know anyone else or speak to anyone else – it's like being cut off from society. I don't speak to anyone, it's the same over again, I belong to him.'

Some of these women were obviously very unhappy. Some had already left again – why did others stay? Isolation, fear of the future and doubts about their ability to manage on their own all played a part. Six of the nine women said that if a house became available for them, they would like to leave their partner again, but four felt they'd be happier doing so if they could share the tenancy with a friend from the refuge:

'I'd have been all right (sharing a tenancy). I like being with someone, because I'm frightened being on my own with the babies, being epileptic, 'cos it can come on any time, see – if I've got the fire on, walking down stairs or anything. I wouldn't have come back to my husband if I'd gone in with another woman, 'cos I was beginning to manage on my own, getting used to not seeing him.'

Summary

The overall impression, then, is that where women had gone back home, relationships had improved only slightly in most cases and the majority of women were still very unhappy. Some had left again, others wanted to but the difficulties of trying to leave in the past and to manage on their own had left women lacking in the confidence to try leaving again, at least for the time being. So long as leaving a violent relationship is fraught with housing and financial problems, it will be an almost impossible step for some women to take, worn down as they have been by years of mental and physical abuse.

12. Looking Ahead

This study examined what provision presently exists for battered women in this country. Its findings show that although the needs of battered women have been catered for in law, there has been a general failure to effectively implement the legislation available. The Housing (Homeless Persons) Act gives women the right to be rehoused if they leave home due to domestic violence. It also empowers local authorities to assist refuges as they are providing accommodation for the homeless. However, women were frequently failing to be rehoused by local authorities and Women's Aid groups were usually offered little support, although they were enabling local authorities to fulfil their duties. The Offences Against the Persons Act and the Domestic Violence Act should provide protection against violent husbands and boyfriends but again the implementation of these Acts was, for the most part, patchy and ineffective. Why were battered women failing to benefit from existing legislation?

Our research indicates that domestic violence was frequently not accepted as a valid reason for women leaving home. Although divorce and separation are now commonplace, ironically, leaving a violent partner is regarded as less legitimate. Response by agencies to women in this survey was often one of disbelief, the woman was thought to be exaggerating or indeed, possibly even to blame for the violence. The violence itself became the focus of attention – whose fault was it, how could it be alleviated – rather than the woman's stated desire to separate. Women trying to leave a violent man were thus having to overcome more obstacles than other women trying to separate.

These attitudes must change if the service to battered women is to improve. Their need is for prompt action from the police when they are assaulted, both in the marital home and after they have

105

separated. They need good temporary accommodation while they negotiate their legal, housing and financial affairs, and permanent housing which takes their needs as single parents into account.

The cost of failing to provide such an escape route is high. Women are forced to suffer violence of varying brutality and live in fear of the next attack. Children are forced to witness the assault of their mother and live in an atmosphere of tension and unhappiness. Other research has shown that violence tends to escalate over time, so prompt action is essential.

At the moment it is organisations like Women's Aid in the voluntary sector, who are meeting the immediate needs of battered women. By providing refuge accommodation and putting pressure on statutory bodies to implement existing laws, they are enabling women to leave violent men permanently. However, to do so, women are having to live in conditions of overcrowding usually for six months and sometimes for over a year. It should not be acceptable for women and children to be forced to live in such conditions to escape violence. Refuges have proved their importance, they are here to stay and something must be done to improve their quality. If local authorities are to fulfil their duty to battered women, it is in their interests to help Women's Aid groups wherever they can both by offering financial assistance, good refuge maintenance and co-operation over women's rehousing.

The cost of the service presently provided to battered women by the voluntary sector is minimal and well below that of providing Homeless Families Accommodation and Bed and Breakfast. Because most refuges are run on the principle of self-help, paid work time is spent on assisting women with advice and information rather than on the practical running of the refuge. Residential wardens and night-shifts are regarded as inappropriate and therefore the cost of staffing refuges is much lower than local authority homeless accommodation. Even if refuges received financial support from local authorities and were maintained in good condition, they would still be an extremely cheap service.

That Women's Aid is providing an essential service to many battered women is evident from this report. However, the strain on voluntary groups to keep refuges open cannot be over-estimated. All battered women who live in refuges are assisted with their legal, housing and financial affairs, all of which involve hours of negotiation with statutory authorities to implement the law. There is a continual need for groups to fund-raise to pay major bills and to replace worn-out household equipment. Refuges need re-decorating at least once a year because of the numbers of women and children living in them, and play facilities and outings for children have to be provided and paid for. Trying to run refuges with inadequate resources was stretching the voluntary efforts of groups beyond their capacity – six refuges have closed for this reason since the survey in 1978. This kind of voluntary commitment cannot be kept up indefinitely. Without better funding, the future of refuges is in the balance. `

Appendix A

Refuge Provision in England*

North East Region
Carlisle
Chester-le-street
Derwentside
Darlington
Durham
Hartlepool
Langbaurgh
Middlesborough
Newcastle-on-Tyne
South Shields
Stockton
Sunderland
North Tyneside
Washington
Wear Valley

Yorkshire Region
Batley and Dewsbury
Bradford
Chesterfield
Doncaster
Grimsby
Halifax
Huddersfield
Hull
Keighley
Leeds
Rotherham
Scunthorpe
Wakefield
Sheffield
York

North West Region
Birkenhead
Blackburn
Burnley
Bury
Bolton
Chester
Chorley
Crosby
Glossop
Lancaster
Liverpool
Macklesfield
Manchester (4)
Oldham
Preston
Runcorn and Widnes
Salford
Stockport
St Helens
Tameside
Warrington
Wigan
Wirral
Wythenshawe

West Midlands Region
Birmingham
Bromsgrove
Coventry
Crewe
Droitwich
Halesowen
Hereford
Lichfield
Nuneaton
Potteries
Redditch
Sandwell
Stafford
Telford
Walsall
Warwick
Wolverhampton
Worcester

East Midlands Region
Bassetlaw
Boston
Corby
Leicester
Lincoln
Loughborough
Mansfield
Newark
Northampton
Nottingham (4)

Home Counties
Aylesbury
Basingstoke
Bedford
Hemel Hempstead
High Wycombe
Luton
Milton Keynes
Oxford
Reading
Slough
South Beds.
St Albans
Stevenage
Watford

East Anglia Region
Basildon
Cambridge
Chelmsford
Colchester
Grays (Thurrock)
Harlow
Havering (Romford)
Ipswich
Norwich
Peterborough
Southend
Great Yarmouth

South West Region
Bath
Barnstaple
Bridgwater
Bristol
Cheltenham
Exeter
Gloucester
Kingswood (Bristol)
Mendip
Plymouth
Salisbury
Stroud
Swindon
Taunton
Torquay
Trowbridge
Truro
Weymouth
Yeovil

South East Region
Brighton
Canterbury
Crawley
Fareham
Havant
Medway
Portsmouth
Reigate
Southampton
Worthing

London Region (South)
Bexley
Bromley
Clapham
Croydon
Greenwich
Lambeth
Lewisham
Merton
Southwark
Sutton
Wandsworth

London Region (North W
Brent
Chiswick
Ealing
Hammersmith
Harrow
N. Kensington
West London
Shepherds Bush
N. Westminster
S. Westminster

108 *Women's Aid refuges rarely now use the term "battered" as it fails to gi
sufficient importance to the emotional and sexual abuse, as well as physic
violence, that women experience.

London Region (North East)

Barking and Dagenham
Barnet
Camden
Clapton
Enfield
Hackney
Haringey
Islington
Newham
Tottenham
Tower Hamlets
St Ursulas
Waltham Forest

Women's Aid Groups trying to set up refuges in England and Wales

Hillingdon
Guildford
Kingston
Leamington Spa
Mid-Sussex
Northumberland
Penzance
Scarborough
Shipley

Welsh Women's Aid

Abergavenny
Aberystwyth
Bangor
Blaenau Ffestiniog
Caernarfon
Cardiff
Cardigan
Carmarthen
Cynon Valley
Deeside
Dolgellau
Llanelli
Lliw Valley
Monmouth
Neath
Newport
North Gwent
North Powys
Ogwr
Pembrokeshire
Pontypridd
Port Talbot
Rhondda
Rhyl
Rhymney Valley
South Clwyd
South Powys
Swansea
Tarian
Torfaen

* This was the most accurate list available at the time of going to press. However refuges are opening and closing all the time so there may be some errors.

The list includes Women's Aid Federation refuges as well as other non-WAFE refuges which may not necessarily operate with the same policies and practices as WAFE refuges.

Appendix B

Table1 : **Where children under 16 were living**

| 80% of children living with father or step-father |

| 11% | living with father or step-father

| 5% | in care

| 3% | living with relatives

| 1% | at other places, e.g. left home, with friends

TOTAL: 1,465 children

Table 2 : Custody position of children aged 16 and under

	Number of Children	Percentage
Mother applying for custody	460	32%
No legal steps taken for custody yet	427	29%
Mother granted custody of children	423	29%
Custody of child/ren in dispute between mother and father	53	4%
Custody of local authority	29	2%
Father granted custody of child/ren	20	1%
Father of children (but ex-husband or ex-boyfriend of mother) granted custody	14	1%
Father applying for custody	8	0.5%
Father of child/ren (but ex-husband or ex-boyfriend of mother) applying for custody	2	0.1%
Others applying or granted custody	22	2%
Total:	1458	100.6%

References

1 R. E. and R. P. Dobash (1980) *Violence Against Wives*, London: Open Books.
2 Del Martin (1976) *Battered Wives*, San Fransisco: Glide.
3 B. Dawson and T. Farragher (1977) *Battered Women's Project: Interim Report*, Dept. of Sociology, University of Keele.
4 R. Chester and J. Streather (1972) 'Cruelty in English Divorce: Some Empirical Findings', *Marriage and the Family*, 34: 706–710.
5 E. Elston, J. Fuller and M. Murch (1976) 'Battered Wives: the Problems of Violence in Marriage as Experienced by a Group of Petitioners in Undefended Divorce Cases'. Cited in R. E. and R. P. Dobash, above.
6 *Report of the Select Committee on Violence in Marriage* (1975), London: HMSO.
7 M. Murch, (1979) 'Privacy and Marital Violence', Dept. of Social Work, University of Bristol.
8 L. Jeffery and J. Pahl (1979) 'Battered Women and the Police', Paper presented to the 1979 Conference of the British Sociological Association.
9 S. Delamont and R. Ellis (1979) *Statutory and Voluntary Response to Domestic Violence in Wales: a Pilot Project*, SRU Working Paper No. 6, University College Cardiff.
10 J. Pahl (1978) *A Refuge for Battered Women*, London: HMSO.
11 D. Kenny and J. Q. Thompson (1978) *Refuges for Battered Women in London – Provision and Need*, GLC Research Memorandum, London.
12 SHAC *Violence in Marriage*, from SHAC, 189A Old Brompton Rd, London S.W.5
13 J. Pahl (1980) 'Patterns of Money Management Within Marriage', Dept of Sociology, University of Kent.
14 M. Finer (1975) *Report of the Committee on One-Parent Families*, London: HMSO
15 T. Farragher (1979) 'The Police and Marital Violence', Dept. of Sociology, University of Keele.
16 M. Maynard (1979) 'The Response of Social Workers to Domestic Violence', WRRC Summer School, Bradford 1979.

111

17 DOE National Dwelling and Housing Survey, (1978) London: HMSO
18 DOE (1973) *Children at Play*, London: HMSO.
19 Joint Charities Group (1978) 'The Implementation of the Housing (Homeless Persons) Act: an Appraisal After Four Months', from WAFE, P.O. Box 391, Bristol, BS99 7WS.
20 A. Arden 'Housing (Homeless Persons) Act Reviewed – Why the Fuss?', *Local Govt Chronicle*, 16 June, 1978, 636–638.
21 I. McConnachie, 'Housing (Homeless Persons) Act Reviewed – The Management Aspect', *Local Govt. Chronicle*, 16 June, 1978. 639–640.
22 J. Melville (1978) 'Domestic Strife; *New Society*, 15 June. 1978.
23 S. Stocking (1981) 'Funding and Facilities for Children in Women's Aid Refuges' from Women's Aid Federation, England, WAFE, P.O. Box 391, Bristol, BS99 7WS.
24 Welsh Women's Aid (1980) *'Mrs Hobson's Choice – a Survey of the Employment Position of Women who have been through Women's Aid Refuges in South Wales'*. Available from Welsh Women's Aid, Incentive House, Adam St, Cardiff.
25 Welsh Women's Aid (1979) *'The Housing Needs of Battered Women in Wales'*, as above.
26 Scottish Women's Aid (1979) *'The Housing Needs of Battered Women in Scotland'*, from SWA, Ainlie House, 11 St. Colne St, Edinburgh.